Florida A&M University, Tallahassee
Florida Atlantic University, Boca Raton
Florida Gulf Coast University, Ft. Myers
Florida International University, Miami
Florida State University, Tallahassee
University of Central Florida, Orlando
University of Florida, Gainesville
University of North Florida, Jacksonville
University of South Florida, Tampa
University of West Florida, Pensacola

The Cuban Treefrog in Florida

Life History of a Successful Colonizing Species

Walter E. Meshaka Jr.

University Press of Florida

Gainesville · Tallahassee · Tampa · Boca Raton

Pensacola · Orlando · Miami · Jacksonville · Ft. Myers

06 05 04 03 02 01 6 5 4 3 2 1

Library of Congress Cataloging-in-Publication Data
Meshaka, Walter E., 1963-
The Cuban treefrog in Florida: life history of a successful colonizing species
/ Walter E. Meshaka, Jr.
p. cm.
Includes bibliographical references and index (p.).
ISBN 0-8130-2109-X (cloth: alk. paper)
1. Cuban treefrog—Florida. 2. Exotic animals—Florida. I. Title.
QL668.E24 M47 2001
597.8'7—dc21   2001034784

The University Press of Florida is the scholarly publishing agency
for the State University System of Florida, comprising Florida A&M
University, Florida Atlantic University, Florida Gulf Coast University,
Florida International University, Florida State University, University of
Central Florida, University of Florida, University of North Florida,
University of South Florida, and University of West Florida.

University Press of Florida
15 Northwest 15th Street
Gainesville, FL 32611-2079
http://www.upf.com

This work is dedicated to Glen E. Woolfenden, teacher and friend.

Contents

Figures

Tables

Preface

This study represents my best efforts to solve a mystery. Something of a biological crime took place. The deed: An exotic species was set loose in foreign lands. The culprit was the Cuban treefrog (*Osteopilus septentrionalis*), the foreign lands were Florida and parts of the West Indies. Some facts associated with the case are relatively well established. Humanity was an accomplice in its dispersal to and within introduced sites, the history of its various introductions was pretty well known, and its geographic range was also well defined. Based on the speed of its range expansion and its ubiquity, the Cuban treefrog was unquestionably a superb colonizing species. The mystery (my dear Watson) is *why?* In the fashion of interesting mysteries, this one is replete with red herrings (was it really predator-free?), victims (native frogs), and even multiple suspects (superior competitive ability and open niche space, to name a couple). In this case, the mystery was real, and the stakes were high.

Worldwide, dispersal of exotic species was not nearly as alarming a phenomenon until transcontinental shipping and exploration dominated the world stage in the 1500s (Di Castri 1989). In present time, the means, motive, and opportunity for this ecological crime have never been so pervasive. Mechanized transport, from automobiles to fleets of jumbo jets, reaches distant places more frequently and faster than ever before. Reasons for dispersing exotic species are as varied as their modes of transportation. Combined, the means and motives of exotic species dispersal provide unexcelled opportunity, and once established they can be monumental ecological disasters. New and Old World introductions of marine toads (*Bufo marinus*), goats (*Capra hircus*), and pigs (*Sus scrofa*), the Nile perch (*Lates niloticus*) in African Rift lakes, and the brown tree snake (*Boiga irregularis*) in Guam are but a few such examples.

At the time of this writing the section of the global neighborhood that concerns the Cuban treefrog is Florida and, peripherally, the West Indies. For the United States, Florida may well be the quintessential exemplar of Man's failure as a steward; among reptiles and amphibians, thirty-nine exotic species have been introduced there with nearly one-half appearing in the past thirty years (Meshaka et al. 2001). Florida's legacy now includes three highly invasive terrestrial plants that are nearly statewide in distribution (Gordon and Thomas 1997), fifty-two exotic species of ants (Ferster and Pruzak 1994), thirty-five exotic species of fish (Courtenay 1997), eleven exotic species of birds (James 1997), nineteen exotic species of mammals (Layne 1997), a mushrooming human population (Browning 1997), hydrological ruination, and the destruction of once widespread habitats. Old-timers watched nature turn into agriculture, and newcomers watch agriculture turn into shopping malls and zero lot line developments, themselves a habitat of sorts overtaking natural ones. Many areas in the West Indies share with Florida simultaneous increase in human population, number of exotic species, and habitat destruction/modification. Indeed, the scales have tipped almost entirely in the opposite direction as millions upon millions of people say goodbye to a vanishing natural world. This is not intended to be alarmist, but rather a simple statement of fact and defense of the position that practices by humans inattentive to their repercussions have created a cascading ecological problem at the local and, by connection and extent, the global scale.

This is the milieu within which the Cuban treefrog excelled over the latter half of the twentieth century and the one in which I have spent a decade counting, collecting, and dissecting the Cuban treefrog and a few other species with the purpose of solving what I found to be a very curious mystery. The reasons for the success of the Cuban treefrog, having both something and nothing to do with humanity, will, I hope, help us to understand why this species succeeded, what its ecological place is in its expanding range, and ultimately what humanity needs to be mindful of in the task of maintaining and restoring intact systems.

Acknowledgments

Many people have been very kind to me in my endeavor to understand something about this species in my dissertation (Meshaka 1994a) and this book, and warrant hearty acknowledgment. I thank Mike Soukup, Dan Foxen, and William B. Robertson Jr. for having cleared a path for my collecting permit in Everglades National Park. I thank Linda Ford (AMNH), Jens Lindum (CAS), George Zug (USNM), Luis Moreno (Instituto, Cuba), Henry R. Mushinsky (USF), Robert Powell (Avila College), and John Simmons (KU) for permission to examine museum specimens. Richard D. Bartlett, Brian P. Butterfield, Pablo Delis, Betty S. Ferster, J. Brian Hauge, Samuel D. Marshall—all, at one time or another, shared in the Cuban treefrog field experience and kicked around neat ideas about colonization and life history. Thanks go to Robert Ehrig (Finca Cyclura, Big Pine Key) and William and Fran Ford (naturalists, Key West) for my knowing a little more about the Cuban treefrog on the Lower Florida Keys, and to Skip Lazell for allowing me to catch Cuban treefrogs at his place (Snake Acres) on Middle Torch Key. I am grateful to Ron Altig, Joseph Collins, Ron Crombie, Robert Henderson, Ernst Mayr, Henry Mushinsky, Robert Powell, Albert Schwartz, Marty Tracey, and Glen E. Woolfenden for enjoyable and fruitful discussions regarding the Cuban treefrog and/or colonization patterns. Work in the Bahamas was made possible and very pleasant by the kindnesses of Hugh and Sandy Buckner (naturalists extraordinaire), William Carey (chief of police), and Pericles Malis (Bahamas National Trust). I thank childhood pal Gregory McTaggart for putting me up during my collecting trip on Grand Cayman Island, Brian P. Butterfield for coming along, and Sister Mary for making us welcome in a local neighborhood where Cuban treefrogs seemingly outnumbered people . . . a frogological dream. Cuba was a most enjoyable experience thanks to the good company of Alberto Estrada, Orlando Garrido, S. Blair Hedges, Luis Moreno, and Richard Thomas. I will fondly remember wading through a lily pond in front of a fancy place while catching Cuban treefrogs with LM, and smoking cigars and enjoying the camaraderie of local folks while catching Cuban treefrogs at night. I thank Archbold Biological Station for employing me while I wrote my dissertation and providing me with museum space for collecting-dissecting-collecting work. I gratefully acknowledge my parents, Walter and Rose Meshaka, who cheer me on and love me so very much. I remain most grateful to my wife, Betty, for her understanding and encouragement from dissertation through postdissertation Cuban treefrog work. I hope it is clear that all of these folks contributed in personal and professional ways to the happy completion of my project, a species and a topic with which I feel fortunate to be acquainted.

|

Introduction

The question

This project began with my first visit to Everglades National Park in August 1990 as a graduate student in quest of a research topic for my Ph.D. This was all very exciting, as it was my first opportunity to see for myself the Everglades so lyrically described by Marjorie Stoneman Douglas (1947) and herpetologically documented by Duellman and Schwartz (1958). I knew that among the exotic species of amphibians and reptiles established in southern Florida, the greenhouse frog (*Eleutherodactylus planirostris planirostris*) was, to some degree, established in the Everglades system encompassed by the park. Because of its ubiquity in southern Florida where I grew up, I was not surprised to see the brown anole (*Anolis sagrei*), another Cuban species, at the park, but I had little more than ever heard of the Cuban treefrog (*Osteopilus septentrionalis*). I had also read that in the park the greenhouse frog was the most successful of these three Cuban species with respect to habitat distribution and abundance (Dalrymple 1988). By these same measures of colonization success, the Cuban treefrog seemed to be the least successful. For this reason, I was very surprised to find so many Cuban treefrogs at a few sites, including the Daniel Beard Center where, five years later, I would find myself employed as curator.

The Cuban treefrog was unusual. I had seen only one live individual before and a few museum specimens, when I took a course in herpetology. Suddenly, I found individuals larger than any other treefrog I was aware of, certainly larger than any of the local native species, which were oddly scarce at the Beard Center. Cuban treefrogs are also warty, altogether a curious looking anuran in an unusual place. Conventional wisdom had it that their large body size and toxic skin allowed them to be predator-free and numerous, like the marine toad (*Bufo marinus*), although this was not my concern at the time. The exotic status of this species was the impetus for my museum-based approach. Beginning in fall 1990 I collected series of them each month; this, for starters, provided information about their gonadal cycle and diet. I collected lightly from the few sites where I knew this species could be reliably found. However, two subsequent field experiences changed my perception of its abundance in the park. First, while exploring Palma Vista Hammock during an afternoon in January 1991, I uncovered groups of individuals under the bark of several trees. It seemed strange to so easily find an animal considered uncommon in natural habitats (Dalrymple 1988). Then, in May, I encountered hordes of mostly male Cuban treefrogs crossing Long Pine Key Road (a.k.a. Research Road) just east of the Beard Center. Males were calling in full force, a call I had never heard before. Many males were in amplexus with females, one another, and individuals of other species, dead or alive. Easily seeing so many of these frogs under bark in the winter and so many of them crossing a road in the summer made me think that this species might be quite a bit more numerous and widespread than previously thought. After much brainstorming, I decided that my "why" question, one that could be answered and one that was very interesting to me, could be phrased as a statement: "the Cuban treefrog is a successful colonizing species, but I don't know why."

The approach

The ecology of a species is indispensable in understanding its colonization success as measured by geographic expansion (Mayr 1926). To understand why the Cuban treefrog has been such a successful colonizing species, I examined six general areas of its biology that were assumed to reflect colonizing abilities: reproduction, activity patterns, habitat affinity, diet, predators, and body size. I compared these selected biological characteristics of the Cuban treefrog with ten ecological correlates associated with successful colonization: (1) high fecundity (Baker 1965), (2) short generation times (Ehrlich 1989), (3) ability to function in a wide range of physical conditions (Mayr 1965), (4) similar habitats in native and introduced ranges (Brown 1989), (5) coexistence with humans (Brown 1989), (6) broad diet (Ehrlich 1989), (7) open niche space (Brown 1989), (8) superior competitive ability (Baker 1965), (9) predator-free space (Pimm 1989), (10) body size larger than closest relatives (Ehrlich 1989). The list of traits for an ideal "weed" species (Baker 1965) includes correlates tested in this study. Baker (1965) was wise to note that a species need not possess all of these traits in order to colonize even large target areas. Although too many confounding variables exist in the colonization process to use these correlates for predicting whether a species will succeed or fail, meeting these ecological correlates increases the chances that the species will succeed in its colonization. Therefore, once the reasons for success are determined, meaningful questions—what is the likelihood of success in other places? what impact is this species having on indigenous species? can this species be eradicated? how if at all can its colonization be prevented elsewhere?—can be more accurately answered.

I treated the ten ecological correlates as a series of null hypotheses, and I chose the southern Everglades, mostly within the borders of the park, as the primary site of the study, for three reasons. First, the immense size of the region shares with the West Indies floristic and climatological similarities. Second, the southern Everglades also maintains a diversity of habitats. Last, this region stands midway between the center of the Cuban treefrog's native distribution in Cuba and the northern boundary of its introduced distribution in mainland Florida. I thought that by comparing colonizing features of its biology in native habitat, introduced sites, and the northern edges of its distribution, I could provide an explanation for its success as a colonizing species, specifically in the southern Everglades and, generally, range-wide.

2

The Cuban Treefrog

Biogeography

What is the Cuban treefrog (*Osteopilus septentrionalis*) and where is it found? It is one of three recognized species of the West Indian hylid genus *Osteopilus,* easily identified by a co-ossified skull. The geographic range of the Cuban treefrog greatly exceeds that of its two congeners. Whereas *O. brunneus* is endemic to Jamaica and *O. dominicensis* is endemic to Hispaniola, the native range of the Cuban treefrog includes Cuba, Isla de Juventud (Isle of Pines), the Cayman Islands, and the Bahamas (fig. 2.1), where it is the only native hylid treefrog (Schwartz and Henderson 1991).

The Cuban treefrog is an exotic species in Puerto Rico, St. Croix, St. Thomas, St. Maarten, mainland Florida (Conant and Collins 1991; Schwartz and Henderson 1991; Powell et al. 1992), Anguilla (Townsend et al. 2000), and (reintroduced on?) Necker Island (Meshaka 1996a). Its status on St. Maarten warrants clarification since first recorded within the past decade. Its colonization pattern on Anguilla was one of existence at barely detectable population sizes for several years, followed by a recent and sudden population explosion (Townsend et al. 2000). Its recent reintroduction to Necker Island is associated with nursery shipments from Florida (Meshaka 1996a). On the lower Florida Keys, this species is presumed to be introduced (Barbour 1931; Schwartz and Henderson 1991), although it is by no means certain that both natural and human-mediated dispersal did not take place in its colonization of the lower Florida Keys (Carr 1940; Duellman and Schwartz 1958; Duellman and Crombie 1970; Trueb 1970; Lazell 1989). Dispersal up the chain of Florida Keys followed construction of Highway 1. By the mid-1940s, the Cuban treefrog was present in Dade County and reported from Miami (Schwartz 1952) and the Everglades (Meshaka et al. 2000) shortly thereafter.

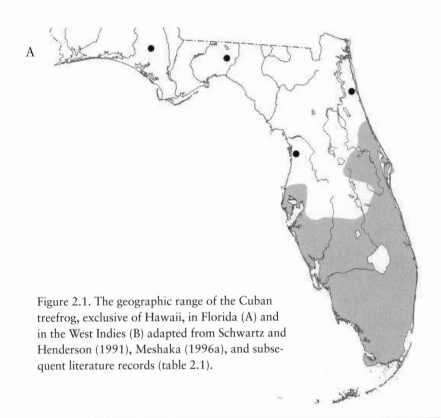

A

Figure 2.1. The geographic range of the Cuban treefrog, exclusive of Hawaii, in Florida (A) and in the West Indies (B) adapted from Schwartz and Henderson (1991), Meshaka (1996a), and subsequent literature records (table 2.1).

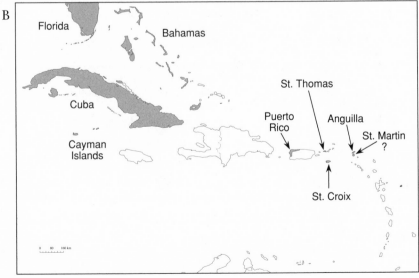

B

Florida

Bahamas

Cuba

Cayman
Islands

Puerto
Rico

St. Thomas

Anguilla

St. Martin
?

St. Croix

0   80   160 km

Table 2.1. Historical records of the Cuban treefrog in Florida.

County	Site	Source
Brevard	County	Meshaka, 1996a
Broward	Dania, Broward	King, 1960
	Broward–Palm Beach Co. line	Lee, 1969
	County	Ashton, 1976
Citrus	County	Meshaka, 1996a
Charlotte	County	Layne et al. (1977), Stevenson (1976)
Collier	Naples, Cape Sable	Duellman and Schwartz, 1958
	Chokoloskee Island	Austin, 1975
	County	Ashton, 1976
Dade	Miami	Schwartz, 1952
	Everglades, Royal Palm	Allen and Neill, 1953
	Everglades	Duellman and Bell (1955), Duellman and Schwartz (1958)
DeSoto	County	Ashton (1976), Stevenson (1976)
Glades	County	Conant and Collins, 1991
Hardee	County	Meshaka, 1996a
Hendry	County	Meshaka, 1996a
Highlands	County	Stevenson, 1976
Hillsborough	County	Meshaka, 1996a
Indian River	Vero Beach	Myers, 1977
Lee	Ft. Myers	Wilson and Porras, 1983
	Ft. Myers Beach	Wilson and Porras, 1983
	Sanibel	Wilson and Porras, 1983
Leon	County	Ashton, 1976
Manatee	County	Meshaka, 1996a
Martin	County	Meshaka, 1996a
Monroe	Key West	Barbour (1931), Carr (1940), Wright and Wright (1949), Mittleman (1950b), Duellman and Schwartz (1958)
	Stock Island	Duellman and Schwartz, 1958
	Cudjoe Key	Lazell, 1989
	Little Torch Key	Lazell, 1989
	Middle Torch Key	Lazell, 1989
	Big Pine Key	Duellman and Schwartz, 1958
	Key Vaca	Peterson et al. (1952), Duellman and Schwartz (1958)
	Matecumbee Key	Wright and Wright (1949), Duellman and Schwartz (1958)
	Upper Matecumbee	Wright and Wright (1949), Duellman and Schwartz (1958)
	Key Largo	Allen and Neill (1953), Duellman and Schwartz (1958)
	County	Ashton, 1976)
Osceola	County	Meshaka, 1996a
Okeechobee	County	Meshaka, 1996a
Orange	Apopka	Conant and Collins, 1991 (record in 1976)
	County	Ashton (1976), Stevenson (1976)
Palm Beach	County	Austin, 1975
Pinellas	County	Somma and Crawford, 1993
St. Johns	County	Krysko and King, 1999
St. Lucie	Port St. Lucie	Myers, 1977
Sarasota	County	Ashton, 1976
Volusia	County	Campbell, 1999
Washington	County	Ashton, 1976

The Cuban treefrog dispersed through mainland Florida rapidly and haphazardly in direction, with most of its geographic range defined by the mid-1970s (Wilson and Porras 1983; Meshaka 1996a; table 2.1). Its geographic distribution is continuous through south-central Florida and slightly farther than that along the coast (fig. 2.1). Disjunct populations in northern Florida are recent in detection and probably in occurrence. Until the status of these populations is evaluated, it remains premature to consider this species widespread within those counties. The temporal and spatial pattern of dispersal through Florida is consistent with human mediation (Meshaka 1996a) and explained by its use of natural and man-made cavities, the former often in the very species of trees commonly used for landscape in developments and along roads (Meshaka 1996a,b).

Thus far, the most geographically remote established colony of the Cuban treefrog is in Hawaii (McKeown 1996), where it has been established on O'ahu since the mid-1980s. The Hawaii population also has the distinction of being the first documented introduction of the Cuban treefrog through the release of pets.

Origin

One step behind biogeography is origin, both of the genus and species. The genus *Osteopilus* is distinguished primarily by features of its cranial osteology and throat musculature (Trueb 1966, 1970; Trueb and Tyler 1974). The close relationship of three species of *Osteopilus* is not in dispute (Dunn 1926; Trueb and Tyler 1974; Hedges et al. 1992; Anderson 1996). Nor is there dispute regarding the closer relationship between the Cuban treefrog and *O. dominicensis* of Hispaniola than between either of these two species and *O. brunneus* of Jamaica. For example, if one examines traits in the life history and morphology of the three *Osteopilus* species (table 2.2), it seems logical to conclude, as did others (Barbour 1910; Dunn 1926; Noble 1927; Myers 1950; Hedges et al. 1992), that the Cuban form is the most generalized and closest to the ancestral stock of the *Osteopilus* group. The Cuban and Hispaniolan forms share the strongest resemblance. *Osteopilus brunneus* is the most differentiated of the three species but shares fewer traits in common with the Cuban treefrog than with *O. dominicensis*. If these conclusions are true, the first *Osteopilus* was probably most similar to the Cuban treefrog. This early form could have first colonized Cuba from the Yucatan or from the South American mainland. Its potentially large body size, both now (this study) and sometime in the past (Koopman and Ruibal 1955), with no apparent specializa-

Table 2.2. A comparison of selected ecological and morphological traits of the Cuban treefrog, *Osteopilus dominicensis*, and *O. brunneus*.

Trait	Species		
	Cuban treefrog	*O. dominicensis*	*O. brunneus*

Ecology

Reproduction

Trait	Cuban treefrog	*O. dominicensis*	*O. brunneus*
Season	Continuous[1]	Continuous[1]	May–September[4]
Site	Temporary pools[1]	Temporary pools, stream edge[3]	Bromeliads[4,5]
Parental care	Absent[1]	Absent[1]	Present[3,5]

Maximum SVL, mm

Trait	Cuban treefrog	*O. dominicensis*	*O. brunneus*
Males	112[5]	80[2]	51[3]
Females	165[6]	100[2]	76[3]

Morphology

Trait	Cuban treefrog	*O. dominicensis*	*O. brunneus*
Dorsum Pattern	Variable[1]	Variable[1]	Variable[1]
Color	Green, grey, brown, black[1]	Green, grey, brown, black[7]	Brown/black to grey[4]
Tubercles	Variable[1]	Few[7]	Absent[4]
Venter Texture	Coarsely granular[1]	Coarsely granular[2,7]	Finely granular at posterior 1/2[4]
Color	White[1]	White[2,7]	Yellowish-tan, brown[4]

Webbing

Trait	Cuban treefrog	*O. dominicensis*	*O. brunneus*
Fingers	Basal[1,8]	1/4[7]	1/4[4]
Toes	2/3[1,8]	3/4[7]	3/4[4]
Digital discs	Large[1,8]	Large[7]	Large[7]
Iris color	Gold[1,8]	Blue[3]	
Forearm texture	Smooth[1]	Smooth[2,7]	Tuberculate[4]
Tarsal fold	Distinct[1,8]	Absent[7]	Weak[4]
Nostrils	Not in terminal position[9]	Not in terminal position[9]	Terminal position[9]
Bone color	Green[3]	Green[1,3]	White[2]

1. This study.
2. Meshaka, unpubl. data.
3. Schwartz and Henderson, 1991.
4. Lynn, 1940.
5. Anderson, 1996.
6. Meshaka, 1996f.
7. Cochran, 1941.
8. Duellman and Crombie, 1970.
9. Myers, 1950.

tion then or now, lead me to propose that the proto-*septentrionalis* could have met little if any habitat or competitive resistance as it dispersed eastward through Cuba before ranging into Hispaniola. Perhaps a founder population accounts for the blue eyes and dearth of tubercles on *O. dominicensis*, even while the species retains a geographically and ecologically broad range on Hispaniola. Perhaps the longer hind legs and greater webbing between toes in *O. dominicensis* are adaptations to a slightly less generalized ecology than experienced in Cuba. In this hypothetical scenario, it makes sense that *O. brunneus* is derived from *O. dominicensis* with which it shares more traits. The proto-*septentrionalis*, if at least as generalized in habits as the Cuban treefrog is today, may have easily colonized Cuba and later the Cayman islands, Isla de Juventud, and the Bahamas with cryptic, if any, differentiation.

In general, two connected but unresolved questions in *Osteopilus* phylogeny are its ancestry and the role of this ancestral group in subsequent speciation events of West Indian hylids. The common ancestor of this group does not appear to be holarctic (Maxson and Wilson 1975), but the identity of its neotropical ancestor is uncertain. Its ancestor is thought to have dispersed from the South American mainland as a member either of the genus *Osteocephalus* (Hedges et al. 1992) or of the *Hyla boans* group (Trueb and Tyler 1974). If *Osteopilus* is derived from *Osteocephalus*, its age of ancestry is early Cenozoic (Hedges et al. 1992). However, karyological data do not support an *Osteocephalus* ancestor (Anderson 1996), and a Central American ancestor that dispersed to Cuba from the Yucatan is equally plausible (Dunn 1926). Consequently, until a full survey of possible hylid progenitors resolves the question of ancestry, age and route of dispersal of *Osteopilus* to the West Indies remains unclear.

The second unresolved problem, as it relates to the origin of *Osteopilus*, is the subsequent speciation events on Jamaica and Hispaniola and the apparent absence of hylid speciation on Cuba. Dunn (1926) proposed that the resident species of *Osteopilus* are the stem groups of native *Hyla* species of those islands. Molecular findings, although incomplete (Hedges et al. 1992; Maxson 1992), do not conflict with those of Dunn (1926). However, osteological (Trueb and Tyler 1974) and karyological (Anderson 1996) data suggest that more than one invasion accounts for the species diversity of the West Indian hylid treefrogs. The answer may well be found somewhere in between the two hypotheses. For example, *O. dominicensis* and *O. brunneus* might account for some, if not all, of the remaining native hylids on Hispaniola and Jamaica. Also plausible is the possibility that speciation has occurred cryptically within the geographi-

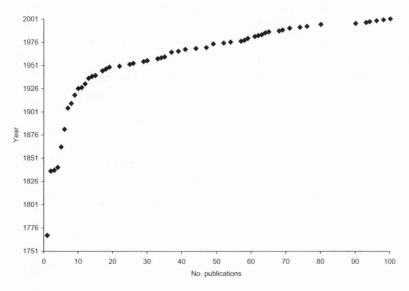

Figure 2.2. An accumulation curve of published papers involving the Cuban treefrog.

cally broad umbrella of the Cuban treefrog. Nonetheless, until a genetic survey examines the relationships among the nine species and the potential for cryptic species within the genus *Osteopilus,* phylogeny of this genus and its role in West Indian biogeographic patterns remains an interesting question.

The major literature

The major literature provided the background information for this study and just as clearly identified the gaps. Over the past two hundred years, the Cuban treefrog has been a subject of 100 published scientific papers; the papers have increased gradually and most notably since the 1950s (fig. 2.2). Studies relating to ecology and distributional records of this species in the United States accounted for the greatest share of works (tables 2.3, 2.4). Most of these works appeared during the latter half of the twentieth century, a time coinciding with its detection in, and dispersal through, the state of Florida. Taxonomy was the third most published topic on this species and was also the topic of the earliest works on the Cuban treefrog. Genetics was the most recent topic to be published on

Table 2.3. A literature review of the Cuban treefrog.

Species Account

Carr (1940), Wright and Wright (1949), Allen and Neill (1953), Duellman and Crombie (1970), Ashton and Ashton (1988), Lazell, Jr. (1989), Conant and Collins (1991), Schwartz and Henderson (1991), McKeown (1996), Meshaka et al. (2001)

Taxonomy and Systematics

Laurenti (1768), Schlegel (1837), Tschudi (1838), Dumeril and Bibron (1841), Cope (1863), Boulenger (1882), Stejneger (1905), Barbour (1910), Dunn (1926), Noble (1927), Barbour (1937), Mertens (1939), Mittleman (1950a), Myers (1950), Jaume (1966), Trueb (1970), Trueb and Tyler (1974), Hedges et al. (1992)

Description and Morphology

Barbour and Ramsden (1919), Noble (1927), Carr (1940), Allen and Slatten (1945), Wright and Wright (1949), Carr and Goin (1955), Conant and Collins (1991), Duellman and Schwartz (1958), Blair (1959), Mittleman (1950a,b), Trueb (1966, 1970), Duellman and Crombie (1970), Trueb and Tyler (1974), Ashton and Ashton (1988), Butterfield (1996)

Fossil Record

Koopman and Ruibal (1955)

Genetics

Goin et al. (1968), Duellman and Cole (1965), Cole (1974), Goin et al. (1978), Hedges et al. (1992), Anderson (1996)

Physiology and Biochemistry

Goin and Jackson (1965), Brown (1969), Maxson and Wilson (1975), Maxson (1992), Wygoda (1982, 1984), John-Alder et al. (1988), Meshaka (1996b)

Distribution, United States

Barbour (1931), Trapido (1947), Wright and Wright (1949), Myers (1950), Schwartz (1952), Allen and Neill (1953), Duellman and Bell (1955), Duellman and Schwartz (1958), Lee (1969), Duellman and Crombie (1970), King (1960), Austin (1975), Ashton (1976), Stevenson (1976), Layne et al. (1977), Myers (1977), Wilson and Porras (1983), Lazell, Jr. (1989), Conant and Collins (1991), Somma and Crawford (1993), McKeown (1996), Meshaka (1996a), Butterfield et al. (1997), Campbell (1999), Krysko and King (1999), Meshaka et al. (2000, 2001)

Ecology, United States

Carr (1940), Wright and Wright (1949), Mittleman (1950b), Lantz (1952), Peterson et al. (1952), Schwartz (1952), Allen and Neill (1953), Duellman and Bell (1955), Blair (1958), Duellman and Schwartz (1958), Neill (1958), Lee (1968, 1969, 1970), Austin (1975), Bowler (1977), Wilson and Porras (1983), Crump (1986), Ashton and Ashton (1988), Dalrymple (1988), Lazell, Jr. (1989), Meshaka (1993), Meshaka (1994a), Love (1995), Meshaka and Ferster (1995), Meshaka (1996a, b, c, d, e, f, g), Butterfield et al. (1997), Meshaka (1997), Meshaka and Jansen (1997), Meshaka (1999a,b), Meshaka et al. (2000, 2001)

(continued)

Table 2.3—*Continued*

Distribution, West Indies

Barbour and Ramsden (1919), Grant (1940), Schwartz (1968), Duellman and Crombie (1970), Schwartz and Thomas (1975), Hedges (1996), Meshaka (1996a), Schwartz and Henderson (1991), Powell et al. (1992), Joglar and Rios Lopez (1995), Kaiser and Henderson (1995), Joglar et al. (1998), Babbitt and Meshaka (2000), Townsend et al. (2000)

Ecology, West Indies

Barbour and Ramsden (1919), Grant (1940), Schwartz and Ogren (1956), Zajiceck and Mauri Mendez (1969), Coy Otero et al. (1980), Coy Otero and Lorenzo Hernandez (1982), Ruiz Garcia (1987), Schwartz and Henderson (1991), Meshaka (1994a, 1996b, 1996g

---

this species. Considering its ubiquity in the West Indies, I was surprised that no life history research had been published, and consider the time to be ripe for studies of genetics and ecology of expanding populations of this species. For the latter topic, Puerto Rico should be a priority, where the Cuban treefrog is the only hylid (Schwartz and Henderson 1991) and a confirmed frog-eater.

Table 2.4. Fields in which studies on the Cuban treefrog have appeared during the period 1768–2001.

Field of study	No. papers (%)
Species account	10(6.6)
Taxonomy/Systematics	18(11.9)
Morphology	17(11.3)
Fossil record	1(0.7)
Genetics	6(3.9)
Physiology/Biochemistry	8(5.3)
Distribution, United States	27(17.9)
Ecology, United States	39(25.8)
Distribution, West Indies	14(9.3)
Ecology, West Indies	11(7.3)
Total	151(100)

Numbers of papers are followed in parentheses by percent of the total. A single reference may encompass more than one topic.

3

The Everglades

The Everglades system

The Everglades is an approximately two- to three-thousand-year-old subtropical and rain-driven system punctuated by distinct wet and dry seasons. Historically, the Everglades began at Lake Istokpoga where, in the "Little Everglades," runoff from the lake flowed southward through the Istokpoga-Indian Prairie Basin to Lake Okeechobee. From there, runoff poured southward and, in teardrop shape, produced over time a rich muck soil deposit beneath the sawgrass marsh. From south of Lake Okeechobee, water, as runoff from the lake and runoff produced locally by abundant rainfall from May through October, naturally flowed more to the southwest, through the Shark River Slough, than to the southeast, through the Taylor Slough. Eventually, the water reached coastal Florida north of Cape Sable on the lower west coast and Florida Bay at the southern tip of peninsular Florida, and flowed out of the Miami River and many small creeks on the lower east coast (Beard 1938; Douglas 1947; Tebeau 1968).

The present-day hydrology of the Everglades is no longer controlled by natural water levels of Lake Okeechobee or rainfall volumes farther south. Two canals, modification of the Caloosahatchee River to the southwest and creation of the St. Lucie River (a canal) to the east, were early but inefficient attempts to control flooding around the lake. After two devastating hurricanes in the 1920s, a dike around Lake Okeechobee was constructed to preserve human habitation and cropland at the south shore of the lake. At approximately the same time, four major canals were constructed to divert water to the east coast, where creeks were converted into canals. Three conservation areas were constructed to hold water between the canals and away from east coast development. Water from the conservation areas is now funneled into the Shark River Slough at a rate that greatly exceeds natural flow rates, through an aperture of the slough greatly reduced in size from its original width. In the middle of the twentieth century, the landscape of extreme southern mainland Florida began to be covered by a web of smaller canals (Light and Dineen 1994), even though as early as the 1930s, human-mediated changes in southern Florida hydrology had already begun to result in a precipitous drop in the water table (Parker et al. 1955; Loftus et al. 1992). Today, the region of the southern Everglades of what is now known as the Everglades National Park is unnaturally inundated with a rush of water in the summer that protects cities from flooding. In the winter, extraordinary use of water by humans results in unnaturally lower water table levels, often one meter lower than the 0.3 meter drop that historically occurred usually at the peak of the dry season.

Everglades National Park

Established in 1947, Everglades National Park, encompassing much of the southern Everglades, is presently a one-million-hectare wilderness containing all the major upland and wetland habitats (table 3.1) of extreme southern mainland Florida and the uppermost portion of the Florida Keys. Among the upland habitats, tropical hardwood hammocks are found throughout the park, sometimes imbedded in pineland but also scattered as islands throughout the vast expanse of sawgrass-dominated marsh. Pinelands are restricted to a series of exposed limestone outcroppings called Long Pine Key. The center of Long Pine Key, farmed since the late 1800s and reclaimed by the National Park Service in the 1970s, exists as forest dominated by the Brazilian pepper (*Schinus terebinthifolius*) and broken in parts, as are the pinelands, by interdigitating finger glades that enable southward flow of water through the key. Mangrove forest borders the coastal fringe of the park, and sandy upland habitat is found in the Cape Sable region of the southwestern border of the park.

Wetland habitats of the park range from nearly permanent, such as sloughs, to the ephemeral, such as muhly grass–dominated prairies of 3–6-month hydroperiods. Sawgrass-dominated marsh forms the largest category of wetland in the park, holding water for approximately nine months of the year. Natural lakes exist at the southern end of the park, and artificial ponds or "borrow pits" occur along the Main Park Road. Buildings are for the most part restricted to the northern (Long Pine Key, Paradise Key, and Parachute Key) and southern (Flamingo) ends of the park. Approximately one million people visit the park each year; this number peaks during the period January to April, with the most visitors in March.

Table 3.1. Plant communities of the Everglades as per ecological classes of Davis (1943), Loveless (1959), and Gunderson and Loftus (1993).

I. Upland Communities—Long Pine Key
  A. Rockland pine forests
    1. Low-stature hardwood understory
    2. Tall hardwood understory
  B. Tropical hardwood hammocks
    1. Mature phase
    2. Successional phase
II. Wetland Communities
  A. Freshwater wetland
    1. Forested communities (tree islands)
      a. Bayheads
      b. Willow heads
      c. Cypress heads
    2. Graminoid associations (marshes and prairies)
      a. Sawgrass marshes
        i. Tall stature
        ii. Intermediate stature
      b. Wet prairies (peat)
        i. *Eleocharis* flats
        ii. *Rhynchospora* flats
        iii. Maidencane marshes
    3. Little or no emergent vegetation
      a. Ponds and creeks
      b. Slough

Source: Reproduced from Gunderson (1994).

Approximately 146 cm of rain falls annually in the Everglades, with almost 90 percent occurring during the period May through October. Winters are mild, and frosts are rare. Most elements of the Everglades fauna are derived from the north-temperate region of North America, but the flora, especially that of tropical hardwood hammocks, has a dominant West Indian origin.

The herpetofauna of southern Florida and Everglades National Park

Duellman and Schwartz (1958) recorded 81 nonmarine species of amphibians (N = 21) and reptiles (N = 60) in southern Florida (table 3.2). Within the boundaries of Everglades National Park reside 63 nonmarine species of amphibians (N = 16) and reptiles (N = 47) (Meshaka et al. 2000).

Table 3.2. Herpetofauna of southern Florida (Duellman and Schwartz 1958) and of Everglades National Park (Meshaka et al. 2000), exclusive of subspecies.

Species	Southern Florida	Everglades National Park
Salamanders		
Amphiuma means	X	X
Notophthalmus viridescens	X	X
Siren lacertina	X	X
Pseudobranchus axanthus	X	X
Frogs and Toads		
Gastrophryne carolinensis	X	X
Schaphiopus holbrookii	X	
Rana capito	X	
R. grylio	X	X
R. sphenocephala	X	X
Bufo marinus[1]	X	
B. quercicus	X	X
B. terrestris	X	X
Acris gryllus	X	X
Pseudacris nigrita	X	X
P. ocularis	X	X
Hyla cinerea	X	X
H. femoralis	X	
H. gratiosa	X	
H. squirella	X	X
Osteopilus septentrionalis[1]	X	X
Eleutherodactylus planirostris[1]	X	X
Turtles		
Chelydra serpentina	X	X
Deirochelys reticularia	X	X
Malaclemmys terrapin	X	X
Pseudemys floridana	X	X
P. nelsoni	X	X
Terrapene carolina	X	X
Gopherus polyphemus	X	X
Kinosternon baurii	X	X
K. subrubrum	X	X
Sternotherus odoratus	X	X
Apalone ferox	X	X
Caretta caretta[2,3]	X	X
Chelonia mydas[2,3]	X	X
Eretmochelys imbrica[2,3]	X	X
Lepidochelys kempii	X	X
Dermochelys coriacea[2,3]	X	X

1. Exotic.
2. Marine.
3. Federally listed.

(continued)

Table 3.2—*Continued*

Species	Southern Florida	Everglades National Park
Lizards		
Gekko gecko[1]		X
Gonatodes albogularis[1]	X	
Hemidactylus turcicus[1]	X	
H. garnotii[1]		X
H. mabouia[1]		X
Sphaerodactylus argus[1]	?	X
S. elegans[1]	X	
S. notatus	X	X
Anolis carolinensis	X	X
A. distichus[1]	X	
A. sagrei[1]		X
Leiocephalus carinatus[1]	X	
Sceloporus woodi	X	
Scincella lateralis	X	X
Eumeces egregius	X	
E. inexpectatus	X	X
E. laticeps	X	
Neoseps reynoldsi	X	
Ameiva ameiva[1]	X	
Cnemidophorus sexlineatus	X	
Ophisaurus attenuatus	X	
O. compressus	X	X
O. ventralis	X	
Snakes		
Ramphotyphlops braminus[1]		X
Python molorus[1]		X
Cemophora coccinea	X	X
Coluber constrictor	X	X
Diadophis punctatus	X	X
Drymarchon corais[3]	X	X
Elaphe guttata	X	X
E. obsoleta	X	X
Farancia abacura	X	X
Heterodon platyrhinos	X	X
Lampropeltus getula	X	X
L. triangulum	X	X
Masticophis flagellum	X	
Nerodia clarkii	X	X
N. fasciata	X	X
N. floridana	X	X
N. taxispilota	X	X
Opheodrys aestivus	X	X

(continued)

Species	Southern Florida	Everglades National Park
Pituophis melanoleucus	X	X
Regina alleni	X	X
Seminatrix pygea	X	X
Storeria dekayi	X	X
Tantilla oolitica	X	
Thamnophis sauritus	X	X
T. sirtalis	X	X
Micrurus fulvius	X	X
Agkistrodon piscivorus	X	X
Crotalus adamanteus	X	X
Sistrurus miliarius	X	X
Crocodilians		
Crocodylus acutus[3]	X	X
Alligator mississippiensis	X	X
Total	84	71

The 55 native nonmarine species of amphibians (N = 14) and reptiles (N = 41) in the park represent a small subset of the 136 native nonmarine amphibians (N = 53) and reptiles (N = 83) of Florida (Moler 1990; Moler and Kezer 1993). With the exception of the reef gecko (*Sphaerodactylus notatus notatus*), the native nonmarine herpetofauna of the park are north-temperate species, most of which are found in the southeastern coastal plain and whose geographic ranges terminate in southern Florida (Conant and Collins 1991). In the nearly fifty years since the study of Duellman and Schwartz (1958), only the eastern spadefoot toad (*Scaphiopus holbrooki holbrookii*) and eastern hognose snake (*Heterodon platyrhinos*) have disappeared from the park and from extreme southern Florida generally (Meshaka et al. 2000).

The center of distribution of three of the eight exotic species in the park, the Cuban treefrog, the greenhouse frog (*Eleutherodactylus planirostris planirostris*), and the brown anole (*Anolis sagrei*), is Cuba (Schwartz and Henderson 1991; Meshaka et al. 2000). All three Cuban species have a historical presence in Florida, and all are widely distributed in Florida (Meshaka et al. 2001). The six other exotic species established in the park are reptiles from the Old World tropics (Meshaka et al. 2000). The Cuban treefrog, apparently missed by Duellman and Schwartz (1958), had been deliberately released in Paradise Key several years earlier (Allen and Neill 1953). Its detection in the lower Keys (Barbour 1931) predated that of

Miami (Schwartz 1952) by at least twenty years, although Archie Jones observed it in Brickell Hammock in the 1940s. By the late 1950s, the Cuban treefrog was present in bathrooms on Long Pine Key and in Flamingo, and the species experienced a boom, as it were, in Homestead during the next decade (Meshaka et al. 2000). At the time of this study, the Cuban treefrog occurred in every major upland habitat, reproduced, at least along the shallow edges of freshwater wetlands, and was considered widespread in the park.

4

Procedures and Organization

In chapter 5, I examined reproductive ecology to test correlates of high fecundity and superior competitive ability that I listed in the approach (chapter 1). Reproductive material from the park was derived mainly from biweekly collections to various sites after dark during November 1990– November 1992, although some specimens were opportunistically collected from their diurnal retreats during daylight visits and a few from surrounding areas. I fixed all specimens in 10 percent formalin and, after at least 30 days, preserved them in 70 percent ETOH. Body length, expressed as snout-vent length (SVL) of preserved specimens, was measured to the nearest 0.1 mm. With stomachs removed and material patted dry with paper towel, I measured the mass of preserved specimens on a triple beam balance to the nearest 0.1 g. Likewise, for both sexes, relative fat mass was expressed as the quotient of fat-body mass, removed from kidneys, over total body mass (without stomach) + fat-body mass multiplied by 100.

For males, length and the width at the mid-point of the left testis was measured with an ocular micrometer to the nearest 0.1 mm. I also recorded the presence of nuptial pads found on what we would consider the meat of the thumb for males in the southern Everglades and from other populations in Florida and the West Indies.

For females, I measured the diameter of the oviducts to the nearest 0.1 mm and I noted the condition of the oviducts, straight or coiled. Four ovarian stages were clearly recognized: I = oviducts < 1.0 mm in diameter, thin and thread-like, ovaries clear; II = oviducts < 1.0 mm in diameter, thin and thread-like, ovaries speckled black with yolking follicles; III = oviducts < 1.8 mm in diameter, coiled, yolking follicles and primary oocytes present; IV = oviducts > 1.8 mm in diameter, heavily coiled, very few primary oocytes present, ova polarized, gravid. Clutch size was estimated by multiplying the mass of the clutch by a subset of the eggs. From each clutch, the diameters of ten round ova were measured to the nearest 0.1 mm with an ocular micrometer. For females of other populations of the

Table 4.1. Study sites within Everglades National Park.

Habitat-Site	Location/duration of study
Disturbed	
1. *Schinus* (SCHIN)	Brazilian pepper forest in Hole in the Donut section of Long Pine Key (December 1991–November 1992). A trail.
Mangrove	
2. West Lake (MANG)	(June 1991–November 1992, October 1995–June 1996). A boardwalk.
Pineland	
3. Pine trail (PINE)	Pine trail preceding and following Mosier Hammock at the Long Pine Key Campgrounds (November 1991– November 1992).
Prairie	
4. Lostman's Trail (PRAI)	Just west of Long Pine Key on Main Park Road (November 1991–August 1992). An overlook.
Tropical hardwood hammock	
5. Gumbo Limbo Trail (HAMM)	Royal Palm Hammock (May 1991–November 1992, July 1995–June 1996). A trail.
6. Mosier Hammock (HAMM)	Long Pine Key Campgrounds (November 1991–August 1992). A trail.
7. Mahogany Hammock(HAMM)	Tree island (June 1991–December 1992, July 1995–June 1996). A boardwalk.
Transitional Pineland/Hammock	
8. Pineland Trail (TRAN)	Long Pine Key (June 1991–November 1992). A trail.

Sawgrass marsh

9. Pahayokee (MAR)   (June 1991–November 1992). A boardwalk.
10. Unnamed overlook   Immediately north of Pahayokee on Main Park Road (June 1991–August 1992). An overlook

Pond

11. Eco Pond (POND)   Sewage treatment pond in coastal prairie, exclusive of trail surrounding the pond (July 1991–November 1992). An overlook.

Slough

12. Anhinga Trail (SLOU)   Traverses Taylor Slough near Royal Palm Hammock on Paradise Key (November 1990–November 1992, July 1995–June 1996). A boardwalk.

Building

13. Daniel Beard Center (HID)   Hole-in-the-Donut on Long Pine Key (January 1991–January 1993, July 1995–June 1996).
14. Iori (HID)   Hole-in-the-Donut on Long Pine Key (June 1991–January 1993, July 1995–June 1996).
15. Garage (HID)   Hole-in-the-Donut on Long Pine Key (July 1991–January 1993, July 1995–June 1996).
16. Long Pine Key Bathrooms (LPKb)   Combined four bathrooms at campground (June 1991–November 1992).
17. West Lake Bathroom (WLB)   (June 1991–November 1992, October 1995–June 1996).
18. Marina (FLAM)   Flamingo (June 1991–November 1992, July 1995–June 1996).
19. Gas Station (FLAM)   Flamingo (September 1991–November 1992, July 1995–June 1996).
20. Fish Hut (FLAM)   Flamingo (June 1991–November 1992, July 1995–June 1996).
21. Post Office (FLAM)   Flamingo (September 1991–November 1992, July 1995–June 1996).

Parenthetical abbreviations relate to habitat type used in diet tables.

A

B

Figure 4.1. The mangrove site of the West Lake Boardwalk before Hurricane Andrew in April 1992 (A) and afterwards in August 1992 (B).

Cuban treefrog in Florida and the West Indies, I staged the ovaries of the females.

Using specimens of *Osteopilus dominicensis* from the National Museum of Natural History, I recorded the presence of nuptial pads on males and staged females with respect to their ovarian cycle. For the green treefrog (*Hyla cinerea*) and squirrel treefrog (*H. squirella*) in the park, I measured testis length and width for males and recorded months in which gravid females were found. The reproductive cycle of the Indo-Pacific gecko (*Hemidactylus garnotii*) from southern Florida was described as

continuous in an earlier paper (Meshaka 1994b), and continuous reproduction in the wood slave (*H. mabouia*) was apparent from examination
of reproductive characteristics of some individuals from southern Florida
(Meshaka et al. 1993). Nonetheless, I tested those findings in collections
and observations of these species in the park.

In chapter 6, I examined development and growth to test correlates of
short generation times, ability to function in a wide range of physical
conditions, and superior competitive ability. Measurements of development began with collections of tadpoles and metamorphoslings in 2 m²
grabs with a dipnet at 21 sites taken every two weeks during June through
October 1991. I made my collection during the hottest times of the day in
order to record the approximate maximum water temperatures. Contents
from each collection were immediately fixed and stored in 10% formalin.
The second step in measuring development was to assign developmental
stages (Gosner 1960) to the tadpoles. I considered metamorphoslings as
individuals possessing four legs and varying degrees of tail reabsorption.
Examination of body size of collected specimens each month in the form
of a scattergram provided a way to estimate growth rates, which I applied
to both the Cuban treefrog and its competitors: green treefrog, squirrel
treefrog, Indo-Pacific gecko, and wood slave.

In chapters 7 and 8, I examined activity and habitat affinity, respectively, to test correlates of ability to function in a wide range of physical
conditions, open niche space, superior competitive ability, similarity of
habitats in native and introduced ranges, and coexistence with humans. I
measured activity and habitat affinity by counting the number of Cuban
treefrogs, green treefrogs, squirrel treefrogs, Indo-Pacific geckos, and
wood slaves observed during biweekly nocturnal visits to 21 sites in seven
habitats (table 4.1, fig. 4.1–4.18). Relative abundance for each site was
derived from the mean value of the higher monthly values. Visits to trails
and boardwalks of natural habitats required approximately ten to fifteen
minutes each. Visits to overlooks each required three to five minutes. Of
the nine buildings, only the bathrooms at Long Pine Key (LPK) campgrounds, Iori building, and Daniel Beard Center (DBC) each required ten
to fifteen minutes of search. During the 1991–1992 sampling period, two
consecutive nights were required to complete a biweekly visit. Census of
the first night always began one hour after dark at Eco Pond and termi-
nated at the prairie overlook just west of LPK. Census of the second night
always began one hour after dark at the Pineland trail on LPK and ended
at Anhinga Trail.

Undoubtedly, flight distances of the Cuban treefrog were greater on

Figure 4.2. The tropical hardwood hammock site of Gumbo Limbo Trail in Royal Palm Hammock before Hurricane Andrew in April 1992 (A) and afterwards in August 1992 (B, C) and in December 1992 (D).

C

D

Figure 4.3. The tropical hardwood hammock site of Mosier Hammock at Long Pine Key Campgrounds before Hurricane Andrew in April 1992.

bright nights than on dark nights, which would have biased my observations in a way that underrepresented number of active individuals. For that reason, I avoided nights when the moon was more than half full. The entire study area spanned 61 km from LPK (Dade County) to Flamingo (Monroe County). Unfortunately, counts were not complete for August 1991, and because of Hurricane Andrew some sites could not be visited in August 1992.

Structural changes occurred on three buildings during 1995–1996. Prior to this period, all seven lights, all 52 air conditioning units, and all awnings were removed from the Daniel Beard Center (DBC). In February 1996, one building light and one parking lot light were reinstalled. During the 1995–1996 season, four of the five lights were absent from the Iori building. Two lights were installed on the garage in February 1996.

At the beginning of each visit, I recorded air temperature with a handheld thermometer (December 1991–June 1996) and recorded relative humidity with a sling psychrometer (June 1991–June 1996). Hourly average of wind velocity (June 1991–November 1992) was available from the DBC. Rainfall records (November 1990–June 1996) were provided by the National Park Service from recorders RPL, RCR, P-35, P-38, and FLA.

A

B

Figure 4.4. The tropical hardwood hammock site of Mahogany Hammock before Hurricane Andrew in April 1992 (A) and afterwards in August 1992 (B).

Figure 4.5. The disturbed site of Brazilian pepper, *Schinus terebinthifolius*, in the "Hole in the Donut" section of Long Pine Key before Hurricane Andrew in April 1992.

A

Figure 4.6. The transitional pineland/tropical hardwood hammock site of the Pineland Trail on Long Pine Key before Hurricane Andrew in April 1992 (A, B) and afterwards in August 1992 (C, D).

B

C

D

A

B

Figure 4.7. The prairie site of the Lostman's Trail Overlook just west of Long Pine Key on Main Park Road before Hurricane Andrew in April 1992 (A) and afterwards in August 1992 (B).

Because wood slaves were concentrated on the buildings at Flamingo, data used for comparisons of general activity with the Cuban treefrog were taken from buildings at Flamingo during July 1995–June 1996. I measured seasonal activity by plotting the sum of the highest biweekly counts for each month from all sites. Calling season was measured by the

A

B

Figure 4.8. The marsh site of Pahayokee Boardwalk before Hurricane Andrew in April 1992 (A) and afterwards in August 1992 (B).

summation of the number of 25 calling sites in chorus that were visited twice each month. Air temperature, relative humidity, and rainfall measured during visits to call sites were used to measure calling activity. On weekdays during May 1995–April 1997, diurnal choruses and volume of rainfall of the day and of the previous night were recorded from the DBC.

A

B

Figure 4.9. The marsh overlook site immediately north of Pahayokee on Main Park Road before Hurricane Andrew in April 1992 (A) and afterwards in August 1992 (B).

To measure seasonal reproductive movements as a type of activity I counted Cuban treefrogs along two roads in the park, driven at night twice each month. All individuals observed on each 8-km transect were counted and the sum of both weeks was used to measure monthly movements and identify peak periods of movements during the year. The first

Figure 4.10. The slough site of Anhinga Trail, which traverses Taylor Slough near Royal Palm Hammock on Paradise Key after Hurricane Andrew in August 1992 (A) and in December 1992 (B).

transect extended from the beginning of Long Pine Key Road to the DBC on Long Pine Key (September 1991–August 1992). The second transect on Main Park Road extended north from Rowdy Bend to West Lake (December 1991–November 1992) and was 35 km SW from the first transect.

In chapter 9, I examined diet to test correlates of open niche space, supe-

A

B

Figure 4.11. Pond overlook site of Eco Pond, a sewage treatment pond in coastal prairie after Hurricane Andrew in August 1992 (A, B).

rior competitive ability, and broad diet. To examine the diet of the Cuban treefrog and its competitors in the park, I collected specimens of the five species at least one hour after dark during the wet and dry seasons of 1990–1992 and 1995–1996. I made certain that the major wetland and upland habitats were represented in this assessment (table 4.1). Stomachs

A

B

Figure 4.12. The Daniel Beard Center on Long Pine Key before Hurricane Andrew in April 1992 (A) and afterwards in August 1992 (B).

were fixed and stored in 10 percent formalin. For the purposes of this study, comparisons were made with prey identified generally no lower than the level of order, the vertebrates being an exception. I measured body length and width of prey to the nearest 1.0 mm and determined dietary niche breadth using Levins' Measurement of Niche Breadth (Levins 1968 in

A

B

Figure 4.13. The Iori building on Long Pine Key before Hurricane Andrew in April 1992 (A) and afterwards in August 1992 (B).

Figure 4.14. The garage on Long Pine Key before Hurricane Andrew in April 1992.

Figure 4.15. One of four combined bathrooms at Long Pine Key Campgrounds before Hurricane Andrew in April 1992.

Figure 4.16. The West Lake bathroom after Hurricane Andrew in August 1992.

Figure 4.17. The gas station in foreground and marina behind it at Flamingo after Hurricane Andrew in August 1992.

Figure 4.18. The fish hut at Flamingo after Hurricane Andrew in November 1992. The post office, unseen in this slide, is to the left of the fish hut and near the Main Park Road.

Krebs 1989). Percentage Overlap (Renkonen 1938 in Krebs 1989) provided a measure of dietary niche overlap. Interspecific comparisons of diet were made using combined sites only from which both species in question were sampled.

In chapter 10, I examined predator diversity to test correlates of few predators. The list of predators of the Cuban treefrog came from three sources: (1) field observations, encounters with predation events occurring naturally; (2) field trials, staged encounters with free-ranging predators; (3) the literature, published accounts.

Last, in chapter 11, I examined body size of the Cuban treefrog across its geographic and habitat range to test correlates of larger body size of the colonizing species than its nearest relatives. To do this, I compared body sizes between populations so as to define its large body size and compared those data to the body sizes of Floridian and West Indian hylids.

Significance values were generally two-tailed unless stated otherwise, and mean values are followed by ± 1 standard deviation. Practically all of the specimens I collected for this study are deposited in the National Museum of Natural History in Washington, D.C. Some specimens are also stored in the Everglades Regional Collections Center (ERCC) in Everglades National Park, Homestead, Florida.

5

Reproduction

Male gonadal cycle

For how many months in a year were male Cuban treefrogs fertile? During both years of the study in the southern Everglades, I found that males could reproduce throughout the year, but the testicular cycle was still distinct and closely associated with daylength (tables 5.1, 5.2). To a lesser degree, the testicular cycle also varied with average monthly maximum temperatures (table 5.2), but not with monthly rainfall or minimum temperatures. The seasonal distinction of the testicular cycle and its strong autocorrelations between years for testis length ($r^2 = 0.81$, $P < 0.001$) and width ($r^2 = 0.87$, $P < 0.000$) meant that in the Everglades, the testicular cycle, having peaked in the warm wet season, was most closely connected with a more stable climatic pattern.

The presence of nuptial pads on the thumbs of mature males provided a reliable external indicator of fertility when compared with the dimensions of the testes (table 5.1). Not surprisingly then, the seasonal variation in the distribution of nuptial pad–bearing males was, like the testicular cycle, strongly associated with daylength for both years (table 5.2). This indicated further that male Cuban treefrogs in the southern Everglades were fertile throughout the year despite a seasonal cycle.

I used monthly frequencies of nuptial pads to measure fertility from other sites for comparison with the southern Everglades and found that males in Florida populations as far north as Okeechobee were also fertile throughout the year. Because the gonadal cycle was dictated by daylength, continuously fertile males in northern populations, like Tampa, although probable in occurrence, would typically exist only in low frequencies during the winter months (tables 5.3–5.6). For that same reason, a greater frequency of West Indian males (i.e., from lower latitudes) were continuously fertile (tables 5.7–5.8). Among its competitors, males of both the

Table 5.1. Reproductive characteristics and fat cycles of 814 male Cuban treefrogs from the southern Everglades during November 1990–November 1992.

Month	Call	Relative testis length	Relative testis width	Relative fat mass	N	Males with nuptial pads	Temp	Rainfall
Nov	0	9.9 ± 0.6	2.4 ± 0.4	2.4 ± 2.7	3	0.0	16.0	2.7
Dec	0	10.8 ± 2.3	2.0 ± 0.7	4.4 ± 2.4	6	0.0	15.0	0.8
Jan-1991	0	10.2 ± 4.1	2.7 ± 1.5	2.8 ± 2.1	6	0.0	15.4	7.2
Feb	0	10.2 ± 3.3	3.2 ± 2.6	2.0 ± 1.7	4	25.0	13.8	3.0
Mar	0	11.7 ± 1.8	2.9 ± 2.7	2.3 ± 2.9	5	20.0	13.6	8.2
Apr	0	14.1 ± 5.5	5.8 ± 3.2	2.3 ± 2.2	7	42.9	18.4	3.1
May	0	20.7 ± 3.7	9.4 ± 1.6	0.6 ± 1.1	41	100.0	19.9	21.3
Jun	0	18.6 ± 3.0	7.6 ± 1.6	1.8 ± 2.2	28	96.4	21.9	27.1
Jul	2	16.2 ± 3.0	6.9 ± 1.6	2.4 ± 1.6	25	84.0	22.1	14.2
Aug	2	19.2 ± 4.8	8.0 ± 1.6	2.5 ± 2.0	17	100.0	22.0	11.2
Sep	8	17.4 ± 3.3	7.0 ± 1.4	1.6 ± 2.3	59	96.6	22.1	39.5
Oct	5	12.6 ± 4.3	4.6 ± 2.2	1.6 ± 1.9	58	56.9	20.8	13.7
Nov	0	9.1 ± 3.0	2.6 ± 1.4	2.2 ± 2.2	46	13.0	17.8	0.6
Dec	0	6.3 ± 1.4	2.1 ± 0.5	3.8 ± 2.8	12	0.0	15.3	2.2
Jan-1992	0	8.0 ± 2.3	2.0 ± 0.9	2.7 ± 2.8	24	0.0	12.5	3.0
Feb	0	9.8 ± 3.3	3.0 ± 1.7	2.3 ± 2.0	16	6.3	12.6	3.7
Mar	2	16.2 ± 2.1	6.5 ± 3.0	1.9 ± 2.0	41	29.3	**12.1**	4.8
Apr	0	10.5 ± 6.2	8.2 ± 2.3	1.2 ± 1.7	26	69.2	15.6	6.1
May	1	19.0 ± 3.9	7.9 ± 1.7	0.5 ± 1.4	64	85.9	14.6	**1.8**
Jun	13	17.9 ± 3.6	7.4 ± 1.8	0.4 ± 1.2	135	95.6	21.6	53.8
Jul	7	18.3 ± 3.8	6.9 ± 1.8	3.1 ± 2.4	29	79.3	22.6	12.6
Aug	5	16.1 ± 3.6	7.1 ± 2.1	2.9 ± 2.3	30	93.3	20.9	15.7
Sep	8	18.1 ± 5.0	6.9 ± 2.0	2.0 ± 2.6	79	88.6	22.8	N.A.
Oct	8	11.9 ± 3.3	5.4 ± 2.3	2.9 ± 2.9	19	57.9	19.5	3.5
Nov	0	9.0 ± 2.1	2.9 ± 1.2	6.0 ± 3.3	34	17.7	19.4	12.9

Mean values are followed by standard deviation. Call refers to the number of call sites from which males were heard calling each month. Monthly mean thermal minima are in °C and monthly volume of rainfall is in cm. Values in bold type represent minima associated with monthly calling records. N.A. = Not available. Males with nuptial pads are presented as a percentage of the monthly sample size of males.

green treefrog (*Hyla cinerea*) and squirrel treefrog (*H. squirella*) were more or less fertile throughout the year (table 5.9).

The relationship of daylength to the gonadal cycle was very interesting to me, especially as it related to other Cuban species. For example, the gonadal cycle of the Cuban brown anole (*Anolis sagrei*) is also predicted by daylength (Lee et al. 1989), and in southern latitudes the brown anole is a continuous breeder (Sexton and Brown 1977). In Miami, breeding is seasonal as this species adjusts to shorter daylength. Although extended

Table 5.2. Correlation coefficients (r) of reproductive characteristics of the Cuban treefrog.

| Parameter | Gonadal cycle | | | |
	Testis length	Fertile males	Male fat cycle	Gravid females
Daylength				
Yr 1	0.83**	0.84**		0.63*
Yr 2	0.92**	0.88**		0.67*
Max air temp.				
Yr 1	0.84*			
Yr 2	0.64*			
Testicular cycle				
Testis width				
Yr 1	0.98**	0.96**	–0.55 N.S.	
Yr 2	0.94**	0.93**	–0.54*	
Testis length				
Yr 1		0.95**	–0.65*	
Yr 2		0.90 **	–0.63*	
Fertile males				
Yr 1				0.71**
Yr 2				0.78**
Female fat cycle				
Yr 1			0.74*	–0.70*
Yr 2			0.81*	–0.47 N.S.

Year 1. November 1990–October 1991.
Year 2. November 1991–November 1992.
* $P \leq 0.05$.
** $P \leq 0.000$.
N.S. not significant.

breeding in Miami under some circumstances was not excluded from consideration, the likelihood of it was less than at lower latitudes. In this regard, territorial displays by males in Homestead occur throughout the year with males battling one another at least as early as February (Meshaka et al. 2001).

The knight anole (*Anolis equestris equestris*) is another Cuban species that is established in Florida. Its gonadal cycle has not yet been studied, but ecological parallels with the brown anole and Cuban treefrog suggest that its gonadal cycle is also influenced by daylight. For example, activity is strongly seasonal (Meshaka et al. 2001; Meshaka, unpubl. data) but

Table 5.3. Reproductive characteristics of 77 female and 51 male museum specimens of the Cuban treefrog collected from Palmdale, Glades County, Florida, during 1993–1995.

Month	I	II	III	IV	%@IV	%Males with nuptial pads (N)	Temp.	Rainfall
Jan	7	0	1	0	0.0	0.0(4)	12.5	9.3
Feb	1	0	0	0	0.0	2.0(3)	13.3	6.8
Mar	2	0	0	0	0.0	0.0(0)	14.7	5.2
Apr	1	0	0	0	0.0	2.0(1)	16.6	9.8
May	0	0	0	2	2.6	0.0(0)	20.1	6.4
Jun	1	0	2	0	0.0	4.0(2)	22.1	27.4
Jul	2	0	3	9	11.7	21.6(11)	22.3	19.8
Aug	0	0	0	1	1.3	2.0(2)	22.7	24.2
Sep	0	0	0	0	0.0	0.0(0)	22.9	15.8
Oct	17	0	2	1	1.3	7.8(6)	20.2	9.9
Nov	8	0	1	0	0.0	0.0(6)	16.6	3.4
Dec	13	1	2	0	0.0	2.0(16)	14.2	2.9
Total	52	1	11	13				

Gravid condition (IV) is presented as the number of gravid females each month as a percentage of the total sample size. Males with nuptial pads for each month are presented as a percentage of the total sample size of males and followed by monthly sample size in parentheses. A five-year average (1990–1994) for average monthly thermal low (°C) and monthly total volume of rainfall (cm) for LaBelle was provided by the Department of Meteorology of Florida State University.

Table 5.4. Reproductive characteristics of 36 female and 24 male museum specimens of the Cuban treefrog collected from Lake Placid, Highlands County, Florida, during 1993–1995.

Month	I	II	III	IV	%@IV	%Males with nuptial pads (N)	Temp.	Rainfall
Jan	0	0	0	0	0.0	0.0(0)	8.5	4.8
Feb	3	0	0	0	0.0	0.0(2)	9.4	6.2
Mar	6	1	2	0	0.0	4.2(6)	11.7	7.6
Apr	2	0	2	0	0.0	12.5(3)	13.8	6.1
May	0	0	1	0	0.0	0.0(0)	16.4	10.9
Jun	4	0	1	2	5.6	8.3(2)	19.5	21.1
Jul	0	0	0	1	2.8	4.2(1)	20.7	22.1
Aug	0	0	0	1	2.8	0.0(0)	21.1	19.2
Sep	1	0	0	0	0.0	0.0(0)	20.4	21.8
Oct	0	0	0	5	13.9	0.0(0)	17.4	10.2
Nov	1	0	0	0	0.0	0.0(4)	12.4	10.6
Dec	3	0	0	0	0.0	0.0(6)	9.4	4.1
Total	20	1	6	9				

Gravid condition (IV) is presented as the number of gravid females each month as a percentage of the total sample size. Males with nuptial pads for each month are presented as a percentage of the total sample size of males and followed by monthly sample size in parentheses. Average monthly low temperatures (°C) followed by monthly averages of volume of rainfall (cm) for Lake Placid were provided by the Archbold Biological Station.

Table 5.5. Reproductive characteristics of 180 female and 114 male museum specimens of the Cuban treefrog collected from Okeechobee, Okeechobee County, Florida during 1991–1995.

Month	I	II	III	IV	%@IV	%Males with nuptial pads (N)	Temp.	Rainfall
Jan	0	0	0	0	0.0	0.0	10.8	5.7
Feb	0	0	0	0	0.0	0.0	11.8	5.8
Mar	14	3	0	0	0.0	7.0(14)	14.3	7.5
Apr	2	3	4	12	6.7	1.8(2)	17.0	5.2
May	3	4	5	16	8.9	19.3(29)	19.7	9.5
Jun	4	2	5	9	5.0	5.2(6)	22.4	17.0
Jul	1	0	6	7	3.9	4.4(5)	23.3	15.9
Aug	1	0	3	4	2.2	3.5(4)	23.4	16.6
Sep	4	1	3	4	2.2	7.0(9)	22.8	14.8
Oct	8	6	6	19	10.6	8.8(20)	19.6	10.7
Nov	7	5	0	3	1.7	2.6(18)	15.5	5.7
Dec	4	0	0	0	0.0	0.0(7)	12.0	3.8
Total	48	24	34	74				

Gravid condition (IV) is presented as the number of gravid females each month as a percentage of the total sample size. Males with nuptial pads for each month are presented as a percentage of the total sample size of males and followed by monthly sample size in parentheses. The thirty-year (1965–1995) average monthly low temperatures (°C) and monthly averages of volume of rainfall (cm) for Okeechobee were provided by NOAA.

Table 5.6. Reproductive characteristics of 87 female and 41 male museum specimens of the Cuban treefrog collected from Tampa, Hillsborough County, Florida, during 1977–1997.

Month	I	II	III	IV	%@IV	%Males with nuptial pads (N)	Temp.	Rainfall
Jan	6	0	0	0	0.0	0.0(4)	10.9	5.6
Feb	6	0	0	0	0.0	0.0(5)	11.6	7.0
Mar	0	1	1	2	2.3	0.0(0)	14.1	7.7
Apr	4	0	1	2	2.3	14.6(6)	16.6	5.1
May	3	5	11	10	11.5	22.0(9)	19.9	7.7
Jun	6	0	3	6	6.9	26.9(11)	22.6	17.1
Jul	0	0	0	0	0.0	0.0(0)	23.6	19.4
Aug	0	0	1	5	5.8	7.3(3)	23.6	20.1
Sep	0	0	0	2	2.3	0.0(0)	22.7	16.5
Oct	0	0	0	0	0.0	0.0(0)	19.0	6.6
Nov	4	1	1	0	0.0	0.0(2)	14.5	4.2
Dec	5	0	1	0	0.0	0.0(1)	11.5	5.1
Total	34	7	19	27				

Gravid condition (IV) is presented as the number of gravid females each month as a percentage of the total sample size. Males with nuptial pads for each month are presented as a percentage of the total sample size of males and followed by monthly sample size in parentheses. Average monthly low temperatures (°C) are followed by monthly averages of volume of rainfall (cm) for Tampa (Wood 1996).

Table 5.7. Reproductive characteristics of 212 female and 180 male museum specimens of the Cuban treefrog collected throughout Cuba during 1890–1993.

Month	I	II	III	IV	%@IV	%Males with nuptial pads (N)	Temp.	Rainfall
Jan	0	1	0	1	0.5	0.0(1)	19.8	7.1
Feb	3	0	1	2	0.9	2.2(12)	19.8	4.6
Mar	11	4	5	0	0.0	1.7(3)	21.0	4.6
Apr	1	0	1	6	2.8	3.9(8)	22.2	5.8
May	0	0	0	4	1.9	2.8(8)	24.0	11.9
Jun	17	4	23	22	10.4	25.0(50)	25.2	16.5
Jul	3	3	3	3	1.4	8.3(16)	25.8	12.5
Aug	7	2	5	10	4.7	16.7(30)	25.8	13.5
Sep	5	2	4	6	2.8	21.1(38)	25.8	15.0
Oct	1	0	0	7	3.3	1.6(3)	24.6	17.3
Nov	0	0	1	0	0.0	0.0(0)	22.2	7.9
Dec	27	12	2	3	1.4	1.7(11)	21.0	5.8
Total	75	28	45	64				

Gravid condition (IV) is presented as the number of gravid females each month as a percentage of the total sample size. Males with nuptial pads for each month are presented as a percentage of the total sample size of males and followed by monthly sample size. Average monthly low temperatures (°C) are followed by monthly averages of volume of rainfall (cm) for Havana (Pearce and Smith 1990).

individuals may be active throughout the year, and winter copulations occur in Miami (Meshaka et al. 2001). Among the exotic anurans in Florida, fertile adult male marine toads (*Bufo marinus*) have been collected throughout the year at locations between Key West and Lake Placid (Meshaka et al. 2001).

Fat storage played a role in the gonadal cycle of male Cuban treefrogs in the Everglades. Production and depletion of fat in males was cyclic and reliably so; the fat cycle autocorrelated between years ($r = 0.66$, $P < 0.02$), ascending at the end of the wet season and beginning of the dry season when prey was still abundant (table 5.1, 5.10). The male fat cycle was contrary to the male gonadal cycle (table 5.2) but was associated in no detectable way with any weather variable in the Everglades. Fat was not examined in its competitors in the Everglades, but in Florida a distinct fat cycle exists in the brown anole (Lee et al. 1989).

Thus, male Cuban treefrogs were continuously fertile from Lake Okeechobee southward, in association with weak but distinct fat cycles. At northern sites, like Tampa, fertility was probably continuous but at very low frequencies during the winter months when fat mass appeared to be greater than in southern populations.

Table 5.8. Reproductive characteristics of 57 female and 102 male museum specimens of the Cuban treefrog collected throughout the Bahamas (Acklin Island, Andros Island, Long Island Rum Cay, New Providence, San Salvador) during 1967–1992.

Month	I	II	III	IV	%@IV	%Males with nuptial pads (N)	New Providence Temp.	New Providence Rainfall	Grand Bahamas Temp.	Grand Bahamas Rainfall
Jan	4	2	30	1	1.8	7.8(24)	18.0	3.6	16.5	5.5
Feb	0	0	0	0	0.0	0.0(0)	18.0	3.8	15.9	5.9
Mar	0	0	0	0	0.0	0.0(0)	19.0	3.6	18.0	8.7
Apr	0	0	0	0	0.0	0.0(0)	21.0	6.4	19.2	3.8
May	2	0	0	1	1.8	19.6(25)	22.0	11.7	21.5	15.3
Jun	0	0	3	3	5.3	2.0(2)	23.0	16.3	21.5	17.7
Jul	1	3	1	0	0.0	13.7(21)	24.0	14.7	24.0	13.5
Aug	0	0	0	0	0.0	0.0(0)	24.0	13.5	24.1	18.8
Sep	0	0	0	0	0.0	0.0(0)	24.0	17.5	23.5	25.1
Oct	0	0	0	0	0.0	0.0(0)	23.0	16.5	21.5	16.4
Nov	5	10	5	3	5.3	3.9(15)	21.0	7.1	19.2	8.2
Dec	7	2	0	0	0.0	2.0(15)	19.0	3.3	17.2	8.0
Total	19	17	13	8						

Gravid condition (IV) is presented as the number of gravid females each month as a percentage of the total sample size. Males with nuptial pads for each month are presented as a percentage of the total sample size of males and followed by monthly sample size. Average monthly low temperatures (°C) are followed by monthly averages of volume of rainfall (cm) for New Providence (Pearce and Smith 1990) and Grand Bahamas (Dupach 1993).

Table 5.9. Mean testis length in mm of the green treefrog and squirrel treefrog in Everglades National Park during June 1991–April 1992.

Month	Green treefrog	Squirrel treefrog
Jun	0.07 ± 0.01; 2	0.11 ± 0.001; 2
Jul	0.06 ± 0.01; 16	N.A.
Aug	0.06 ± 0.02; 4	0.07 ± 0.00; 1
Sep	0.06 ± 0.02; 17	0.08 ± 0.03; 5
Oct	0.06 ± 0.01; 2	0.06 ± 0.01; 5
Nov	0.07 ± 0.003; 2	0.08 ± 0.04; 6
Dec	N.A.	0.08 ± 0.02; 8
Jan-1992	N.A.	0.08 ± 0.00; 1
Feb	N.A.	0.07 ± 0.01; 5
Mar	0.05 ± 0.01; 2	0.09 ± 0.02; 5
Apr	N.A.	0.08 ± 0.00; 1

Mean followed by ± 2 standard deviations and sample size. N.A. = Not available.

Table 5.10. Number of arthropods counted one night each month in a 2 x 2 m quadrant on the lighted and unlighted portions of the Daniel Beard Center in Everglades National Park during January–December 1992.

Month	Lighted	Dark
Jan	9	0
Feb	10	1
Mar	9	0
Apr	10	0
May	70	0
Jun	205	0
Jul	400	0
Aug	450	0
Sep	250	0
Oct	40	0
Nov	20	0
Dec	3	0

Table 5.11. Correlation coefficients (r) between monthly number of sites in chorus and monthly weather values in Everglades National Park.

	No. sites in chorus each month
Vol. rain	0.88, $P < 0.000$
Average min. temp.	0.65, $P < 0.006$
Average max. temp.	0.64, $P < 0.006$

Male calling

Males called throughout the year in the southern Everglades, but in the park I heard nocturnal calling during March through October and most frequently during June through October (table 5.1). The number of sites in chorus was closely associated with monthly volume of rainfall and mean monthly thermal minima and maxima (table 5.11). The number of months in which nocturnal choruses were heard was limited by monthly volume of rainfall of at least 1.8 cm (March–October, January). Thermal constraints to calling in the southern Everglades were weak. Males called during the coldest months of the year, when monthly temperature lows were 12.1 °C (table 5.1). Calling was heard in December and January 1998 and January 2000.

Calling generally began one to two hours after sunset and became more noticeable four to five hours after sunset. If eggs were laid, calling peaked in its intensity just before sunrise, and during sustained calling, choruses seemed to take on a cadence of sorts. Generally speaking, calling was strongly associated with warm, wet weather. Males called at night when conditions were calm or windy and often associated with rain, but always when humidity was high and air temperatures were warm (table 5.12). Males did not call in hard rain but remained silent until rainfall ceased or reduced to drizzling between bouts, at which time loud raucous choruses broke out. Volume of rain associated with nocturnal calling was high (table 5.11, 5.12); however, volume of rain the day of nocturnal calling was significantly greater ($X^2_{df = 6} = 17.92$, $P < 0.00$) than the volume of rain of the day before nocturnal calling.

Males called infrequently during the day between May and October after heavy rainfall. During low-pressure systems, like Hurricane Andrew, Hurricane Georges, and Tropical Storm Harvey, males called intermittently throughout the day. The volume of rainfall the night before a diurnal chorus was significantly greater than volume of rainfall the day of a diurnal chorus. Nocturnal calling required greater volume of rainfall than did diurnal calling whether the rain fell the day of or the night before a chorus (table 5.13).

As in the southern Everglades, rainfall was the overwhelming stimulus for calling in Cuban populations. For example, the morning after a sudden and severe daytime storm (*manga de viento*) in Havana during June 1993, eggs were found in abundance in the stone pools in front of the Palacio de las Convenciones. Even a poor imitation of their call elicited a strong reply by males that remained hidden in crevices of the statues.

Table 5.12. Physical parameters associated with activity of the Cuban treefrog in Everglades National Park.

Parameters	Cuban treefrog	Green treefrog	Squirrel treefrog	Indo-Pacific gecko
General activity				
Nature and buildings				
Air temp.	23.7 ± 5.6; 9.5–31.5; 1,992	22.6 ± 4.0; 14.0–30.0; 356	22.2± 4.4; 12.0–31.5; 660	25.2 ± 2.9; 16.0–30.0; 939
Relative humidity	94.5 ± 5.3; 65–100; 1,870	89.8 ± 8.3; 65–100; 252	93.2 ± 5.4; 65–100; 293	85.0 ± 10.0; 65–100; 280
Rainfall	1.2 ± 2.1; 0.0–12.9; 3,117	0.7 ± 1.7; 0.0–12.9; 481	0.3 ± 1.0; 0.0–8.4; 890	0.8 ± 2.2; 0.0–12.9; 361
Nature				
Air temp.	23.9 ± 3.0; 13.0–20.0; 525			
Buildings				
Interior/exterior				
Air temp.	21.4 ± 2.9; 10.0–27.5; 195			
Exterior only				
Air temp.	24.0 ± 6.6; 9.5–31.5; 1,272			
Wind velocity	5.6 ± 1.8; 0.97–18.0; 939			
Calling activity				
Nocturnal				
Air temp.	25.7 ± 2.0; 21.5–30.0; 68	25.6 ± 2.0; 21.5–30.0; 73	25.5 ± 1.8; 23.0–30.0; 44	
Wind velocity	8.7 ± 5.9; 2.72–18.0; 5			
Relative humidity	97.8 ± 3.5; 81–100; 72	95.0 ± 7.7; 65–100; 78	97.8 ± 3.0; 86–100; 49	
Rainfall				
That day	3.0 ± 2.9; 0.00–12.9; 68	1.5 ± 2.4; 0.0–12.9; 83	2.4 ± 1.2; 0.0–12.9; 49	
Night before	1.3 ± 2.2; 0.00–13.0; 74			
Diurnal				
Rainfall				
That day	0.8 ± 1.3; 0.0–4.2; 10			
Night before	3.3 ± 2.3; 0.0–7.4; 10	0.3 ± 0.3; 0.0–0.6; 2	2.1 ± 1.6; 0.0–5.6; 12	
Movements				
Air temp.	26.4 ± 1.7; 22.0–29.0; 355			
Rainfall	4.2 ± 3.3; 0.0–8.4; 602			
Oviposition				
Min. air temp.	23.8 ± 1.5; 19.0–26.9; 36			
Rainfall	4.8 ± 5.8; 0.0–25.6; 25			

Mean values of air temperature (°C), wind velocity (km/hr), relative humidity (%), and volume of rainfall (cm), are followed by standard deviations, range of values, and sample size.

Table 5.13. Statistical comparisons of volume of rainfall associated with nocturnal and diurnal calling in the Cuban treefrog in Everglades National Park.

	Vol. rain day of diurnal chorus	Vol. rain night before nocturnal chorus
Vol. rain night before diurnal chorus	$F = 3.09$, $P < 0.03$, $T_{df = 18} = -2.46$, $P < 0.02$	$T_{df = 3,132} = -19.76$, $P < 0.000$
Vol. rain day of nocturnal chorus	$F = 5.00$, $P < 0.001$, $T_{df = 3,229} = 5.68$, $P < 0.000$	

When I compared the threshold monthly values for temperature (12.1 °C) and rainfall (1.8 cm) associated with calling in the Everglades ($\pm$ 0.3 °C and 1.3 cm, respectively) with historical values from other localities (see Burton [1994] for the Cayman Islands), I found that populations throughout the West Indies, Hawaii, and in Florida north to the southern shore of Lake Okeechobee were continuous callers, even if punctuated with strongly seasonal amplitudes of calling activity (table 5.14). In Palmdale, February and March choruses have been heard by residents, and I heard males calling in December 1994. North of Palmdale to Orlando, the predicted calling season was limited almost uniformly to the period March–November, and in Lake Placid, from late March to early November. At all of these sites, calling season was enforced by low temperatures. Thus for much of its introduced range in Florida the Cuban treefrog was weakly constrained in its calling season despite strong seasonal amplitudes.

In the park, calling seasons were shorter for the green treefrog and the squirrel treefrog (*H. squirella*), which were heard during February–October and March–October, respectively. However, during the study, calling by both species was heard during April–September when average monthly minimum temperature was above 15.0 °C. If allowance is made for a $\pm$ 0.3 °C and 1.3 cm variation from the average values of monthly temperature lows and precipitation associated with calling, the historic calling season for these species in Miami is continuous, with strong summer seasonal amplitudes (table 5.15).

Among the exotic species of amphibians, the marine toad has a calling season pattern similar to that of the Cuban treefrog. In Miami, marine toads normally call during January–October (Krakauer 1968), but occasionally do so year-round (Meshaka et al. 2001). In Lake Placid, Florida, calling records exist during January–September (Meshaka et al. 2001). Based on threshold rainfall and temperature values associated with call-

Table 5.14. Summary of most probable calling and egg-laying seasons for the Cuban treefrog from sites in Florida and Cuba as predicted by weather conditions associated with those activities.

Location	Season Calling	Oviposition
Florida		
Orlando	March–November	May–October
Tampa	March–December	May–October
Lake Placid	April–November	June–October
Okeechobee	March–November	May–October
Palmdale	Continuous	May–October
Southern Everglades	Continuous	March–November
Key West	Continuous	Continuous
Bahamas		
New Providence	Continuous	March–November
Grand Bahamas	Continuous	March–September
Cuba		
Havana	Continuous	Continuous
Cayman Islands	Continuous	May–November
Hawaii		
Honolulu	Continuous	Continuous
Puerto Rico		
San Juan	Continuous	Continuous

Table 5.15. Number of sites in chorus and presence of gravid females of the green treefrog and squirrel treefrog in Everglades National Park during July 1991–September 1992.

Month	Green treefrog Call sites	Gravid females	Squirrel treefrog Call sites	Gravid females
Jul	3		2	
Aug	2		1	
Sep	7	X	4	X
Oct	0		0	
Nov	0		0	
Dec	0		0	
Jan 1992	0		0	
Feb	0		0	
Mar	0		0	X
Apr	2	X	1	
May	0		0	
Jun	14	X	13	X
Jul	9		2	X
Aug	2	X	0	X
Sep	4	X	5	

ing, the calling season for this species in Lake Placid normally does not extend beyond October, but calling is possible year round. The calling season of the greenhouse frog (*Eleutherodactylus planirostris planirostris*) is also longest in extreme southern Florida. Whereas in Gainesville, Florida, calling is heard during April–September (Goin 1947), calling was heard during March–October in the park and during February–November at my residence in Homestead.

Besides knowing when the Cuban treefrog called, I also wanted to know from where it called, as another measure of overlap with its potential competitors. Males called from the ground to heights of about three meters at all calling sites except the long hydroperiod systems of slough, pond, and marsh. They never floated in the water to call but crowded on twigs a few centimeters above the water line and at the water's edge or called from water shallow enough that they were sitting. During the days and nights surrounding breeding events, choruses could often be induced by imitating their call. Under cool and/or dry conditions and between breeding events during the wet season, males reticently returned my call with a series of clicks or a slower version of their characteristic grating squawk, followed by three to five slow clicks. However, this species was shy of light, even during major breeding events, and movements of large shadows or the use of lights halted calling.

Among its competitors in the park, the green treefrog was heard calling from flooded fields, although calling males were recorded primarily from long hydroperiod systems such as lakes, ponds, sloughs, and marshes near upland connection. Despite some overlap with the green treefrog, the squirrel treefrog called in more of the same types of short hydroperiod places as the Cuban treefrog. Examples included finger glades, flooded fields, and depressions in Brazilian pepper stands; however, unlike the Cuban treefrog, the squirrel treefrog also called from sawgrass marsh.

The marine toad shares with the Cuban treefrog the ability to call from and reproduce in ephemeral systems that typify disturbed habitats in Florida. However, unlike the Cuban treefrog, this species frequently calls from permanent systems that contain predatory fish (Meshaka et al. 2001).

Female gonadal cycle

In the southern Everglades, females were gravid throughout the year (table 5.16) but were most frequently gravid during the wet season. For both years, monthly distribution of gravid females was closely associated with daylength (table 5.2), and equivocally so with monthly volumes of rainfall

Table 5.16. Gonadal (N = 988) and fat (N = 832) cycles of female Cuban treefrogs during November 1990–November 1992 in the southern Everglades.

Month	I	II	III	IV	%@IV	%Fat (N)
Nov	17	2	0	0	0.0	2.5 ± 1.3 (N = 17)
Dec	27	0	0	0	0.0	4.0 ± 2.6 (N = 23)
Jan-1991	2	1	0	0	0.0	2.1 ± 0.4 (N = 2)
Feb	2	5	2	0	0.0	2.7 ± 1.0 (N = 8)
Mar	6	1	1	0	0.0	1.6 ± 1.4 (N = 3)
Apr	3	4	13	3	13.0	0.8 ± 1.1 (N = 21)
May	0	1	4	17	77.3	0.1 ± 0.5 (N = 23)
Jun	18	10	19	8	14.6	0.6 ± 1.4 (N = 45)
Jul	12	5	11	12	30.0	0.7 ± 1.2 (N = 37)
Aug	10	3	12	8	24.2	0.9 ± 1.8 (N = 27)
Sep	37	4	8	13	21.0	0.9 ± 1.5 (N = 38)
Oct	53	16	11	2	2.4	1.9 ± 1.9 (N = 57)
Nov	21	9	4	1	2.9	2.4 ± 2.5 (N = 30)
Dec	34	12	4	0	0.0	2.5 ± 2.8 (N = 38)
Jan-1992	11	9	3	1	4.2	2.1 ± 2.3 (N = 18)
Feb	24	18	5	2	4.1	1.9 ± 1.1 (N = 40)
Mar	18	21	6	5	10.0	1.4 ± 1.6 (N = 40)
Apr	9	7	9	9	26.5	0.8 ± 1.5 (N = 31)
May	25	2	14	10	19.6	0.6 ± 1.7 (N = 44)
Jun	19	8	17	21	32.3	0.4 ± 1.5 (N = 58)
Jul	19	6	11	22	37.9	1.4 ± 2.2 (N = 57)
Aug	8	8	13	3	9.4	1.7 ± .1 (N = 32)
Sep	20	10	11	26	38.8	2.0 ± 2.6 (N = 61)
Oct	27	7	2	13	26.5	2.3 ± 2.5 (N = 47)
Nov	15	5	15	6	14.6	2.6 ± 2.2 (N = 35)
Total	437	174	195	182		

Gravid (IV) females are presented as a percentage of the monthly total of females.

and the monthly average values of temperature highs and lows. However, the gravid condition, essentially continuous, was present in months of at least 1.8 cm total volume of rainfall and of a mean temperature low not less than 12.1 °C. For both years, monthly distribution of gravid females overlapped that of males bearing nuptial pads, indicating that synchrony in fertility existed between the sexes (table 5.2).

Despite small sample sizes, the presence of nearly gravid females (stage III) during the winter months in Palmdale and Tampa suggested that at least some females are capable of laying eggs throughout the year, as in other Florida sites (tables 5.3–5.6). Continuous fertility in female Cuban treefrogs, as identified by gravid individuals, was apparent in populations across the West Indies (tables 5.7, 5.8).

Among the native competitors, continuous fertility was not apparent in females of the green treefrog (April–September) and squirrel treefrog (to October in 1996) in the park. The gravid condition in both native species was shorter than that of the Cuban treefrog, overlapping the April–September calling season of the study. Its other competitors, the Indo-Pacific gecko (*Hemidactylus garnotii*) and wood slave (*H. mabouia*), were gravid throughout the year in the park. The Indo-Pacific gecko is also a continuous breeder in south-central Florida (Meshaka 1994b). Elsewhere in Florida, the Mediterranean gecko (*H. turcicus*), once a ubiquitous species on buildings, is constrained by seasonal egg-laying (Meshaka 1995). It is thought that its shorter breeding season has hastened its demise in the face of more fecund and successful congeners (Meshaka 1995; Meshaka et al. 2001).

Among the exotic anurans, the marine toad also is gravid throughout the year in Miami (Meshaka et al. 2001). The dearth of Lake Placid specimens during November–February precluded an assessment of fertility; however, gravid and nearly gravid females were present in all remaining months.

Female body fat increased in mass near the end of the wet season and beginning of the dry season, a time when the frequencies of gravid females (table 5.16) and breeding males (table 5.1) were on the decline. Fat was rapidly depleted from the latter half of the dry season through the middle of the wet season, when most females converted energy into clutch production. In this connection, fat was greater in mass ($F = 2.79$, $P < 0.0000$; $t_{df=487} = -10.08$, $P < 0.0000$) in nongravid females (1.8 ± 2.2 %; $0.0–14.5$; $N = 651$) than in gravid counterparts (0.5 ± 1.3 %; $0.00–10.0$; $N = 181$), which were forced to rely on direct conversion of energy into clutch production after the first clutches of the season.

The seasonality of the female fat cycle was fixed and autocorrelated between years ($r = 0.78$, $P < 0.003$) and overlapped the fat cycle of males for both years (table 5.2). Consequently, female fat used for egg production reached its peak just before the beginning of the breeding season. The timing of the fat cycle and its role in clutch production early in the breeding season may have accounted for the production of larger clutches, independent of female body size, at the beginning of the 1991 and 1992 egg-laying seasons than during the intervening winter months (hurricane section).

Clutch characteristics and oviposition

The clutches produced by the Cuban treefrog from the southern Everglades were potentially very large ($3,961 \pm 2,211.8$; $1,177–16,371$; $N =$

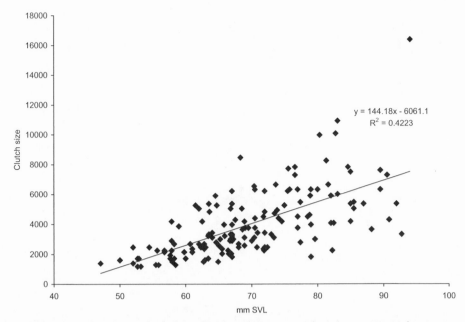

Figure 5.1. The relationship of clutch size with snout-vent length (mm SVL) of 153 Cuban treefrogs (69.5 ± 10.0; 47.1–94.0) in the southern Everglades during November 1990–November 1992. F = 150.88, p < 0.000.

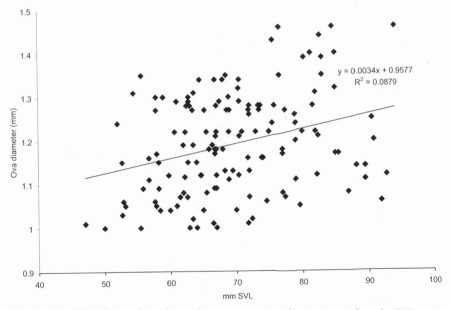

Figure 5.2. The relationship of ova diameter (mm) with snout-vent length (SVL mm) of 147 Cuban treefrogs (69.5 ± 10.2; 47.1–94.0) in the southern Everglades during November 1990–November 1992. F = 14.70, p < 0.0002.

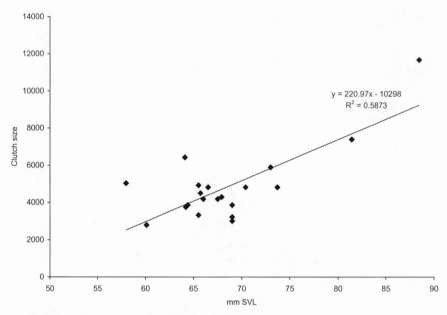

Figure 5.3. The relationship of clutch size with snout-vent length (SVL mm) of 20 Cuban treefrogs (68.5 + 6.6 mm SVL; 58.0–88.4; 20) from Okeechobee where F = 25.60; p < 0.000.

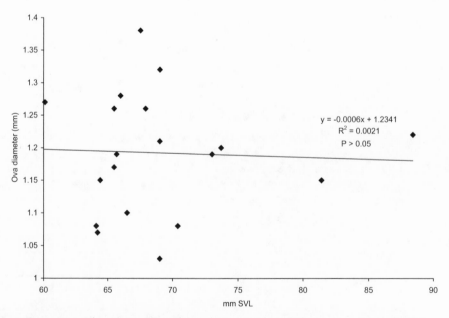

Figure 5.4. The relationship of ova diameter (mm) with snout-vent length (SVL mm) of 20 Cuban treefrogs (68.5 + 6.6 mm SVL; 58.0–88.4) from Okeechobee.

153). Both the clutch size and mean ova diameter (1.2 ± 0.2 mm; 1.0–1.5; N = 1,470) covaried with female body size such that female body size explained 42 percent of the variance of clutch size (fig. 5.1) and 9 percent of the variance of ova diameter (fig. 5.2). Large clutches were also produced in Okeechobee, Florida, where body size explained 59 percent of the variation in potentially large ($4,831.1 \pm 1,920$; 2,782–11,663; N = 20) clutch sizes (fig. 5.3); however, body size did not explain any of the variation in ova diameter (1.19 ± 0.09 mm; 1.03–1.38) in that population (fig. 5.4).

Largest clutch sizes of its hylid competitors were at best on par with the minimum clutch size of the Cuban treefrog. For example, in south-central Florida the green treefrog (51.7 ± 3.5 mm SVL; N = 11) lays clutches ($2,591.2 \pm 1,151.9$; N = 11) that are on average less than 70 percent of the clutch size laid by Cuban treefrogs in south-central Florida and the southern Everglades. The squirrel treefrog (38.0 ± 0.8 mm SVL; N = 3), also from south-central Florida, lays clutches ($1,068.3 \pm 184.6$; N = 3) that are even smaller than those of the Cuban treefrog. Clutch sizes of both geckos in the park are never more than two eggs at a time, which puts these species at a reproductive disadvantage even if they live long lives. In the case of the Indo-Pacific gecko, continuous production of up to three clutches annually is possible by all adults of this all-female species (Kluge and Eckhardt 1969; Voss 1975; Meshaka 1994b, 2000). Up to four clutches of hard-shelled eggs are possible annually in *H. mabouia* (Meshaka et al. 1993; Meshaka 1994b).

The ability to produce large clutches of large eggs throughout the year produces a distinct advantage in the colonization process of the species by minimizing or eliminating the wait to reproduce after arriving at a site. However, the true measure of this advantage is found in the actual egg-laying season. Put another way: for all their *potential* fecundity, when are females *actually* laying all of these enormous clutches? In all my wandering and collecting, observations of clutches in nature were rare, and so timing of most clutch depositions was almost exclusively approximated by the collection of very young tadpoles. Luckily for me, Cuban treefrogs were abundant around my residence in Homestead, *and* females liked to lay their eggs in my swimming pool, where I could easily find them. In fact, on more than one occasion, I found exhausted postreproductive females hauling themselves out of the swimming pool at daybreak, covered with eggs and sometimes with the male still hanging on.

Seeing this as an opportunity to identify the weather constraints on actual egg deposition, I monitored the pool each morning for eggs during 1997–1999. In 1997, eggs were laid during April–October, when monthly

Table 5.17. Egg-laying activity of the Cuban treefrog from a residential swimming pool in Homestead in 1998.

| Month | No. breeding nights | 1998 | | Average | |
		Min. air temp.	Rainfall	Min. air temp.	Rainfall
Jan	0	17.1	1.7	15.1	5.1
Feb	0	16.0	11.8	15.5	4.9
Mar	0	16.0	11.3	17.6	6.0
Apr	0	18.5	0.3	19.7	9.1
May	3	20.9	10.1	21.8	15.1
Jun	2	23.9	7.1	23.7	21.8
Jul	6	24.0	12.6	24.5	16.8
Aug	12	24.4	17.2	24.6	18.8
Sep	8	N.A.	26.8	24.6	18.8
Oct	6	21.7	6.7	22.1	17.5
Nov	3	18.7	13.4	19.0	7.6
Dec	0	16.7	0.9	16.2	4.5

The 1998 average monthly thermal low (°C) and monthly total volume of rainfall (cm) for Homestead were provided by NOAA. N.A. = Not available. Long-term weather parameters for Miami are provided from Wood (1996).

volume of rainfall was at least 4.1 cm and average monthly thermal low was at least 19.4 °C. I repeated this in 1998 and found eggs during May–November (table 5.17) when monthly volume of rainfall was at least 6.7 cm and average monthly thermal low was at least 18.7 °C. In 1999, eggs were laid in the swimming pool during April–October, when the monthly volume of rainfall was at least 2.3 cm and the average monthly low was at least 17.6 °C.

As all of this related to nightly egg-laying activity, I found that the volume of nightly rainfall associated with oviposition, nearly 5.0 cm on average (table 5.12), was significantly higher ($P < 0.05$) than that associated with calling. Eggs were never laid when nightly thermal lows were below 20 °C. In all three years, egg-laying seasons were subsumed by the March–November calling season. Essentially, more so than temperature, rainfall played the principal role in the reproductive activities of the Cuban treefrog.

At last, with threshold values of rainfall (± 1.3 cm) and average minimum temperatures (± 0.3 °C) associated with calling in the Everglades

(1.8 cm and 12.1 °C, respectively) and egg laying in Homestead (2.3 cm and 17.6 °C, respectively), long-term weather data for Miami predicted that extreme southern Everglades populations of the Cuban treefrog historically laid their eggs during March–November, generally avoiding three cold winter months (table 5.17). Not surprisingly, my earliest records of egg laying (April 1997 and 1999) were at the very end of the month and my latest records (November 1998) were near the beginning of the month. Even a cursory look at the predicted egg-laying seasons (table 5.14) and the long-term weather data for the various sites (tables 5.3–5.8, 5.16–5.18) disclosed two trends. First, egg-laying seasons of mainland Florida populations were defined by temperature, whereas those of insular sites were defined by rainfall. For example, despite similarity of latitudes, the breeding season in Okeechobee was longer than that of Lake Placid, perhaps because of the warmth afforded by Lake Okeechobee at the former site. In that regard, the coastal city of Tampa provided conditions for a longer breeding season than the interior town of Lake Placid, located nearly 90 km southward. Second, the egg-laying season of the Cuban treefrog in the southern Everglades was more similar to that of the West Indies and Hawaii, than to Florida sites north of Palmdale.

The long calling season of the Cuban treefrog was equated with a long egg-laying season in the southern Everglades, and both exceeded in length those of its hylid competitors. However, it remained quite capable of reproducing during other times of the year, under the right conditions, which become increasingly unlikely as one ventures away from southern Florida and Cuba. In northern sites like Tampa and Orlando, the Cuban treefrog is just another summer breeding anuran (like its hylid competitors throughout Florida).

Although clutch size of the Cuban treefrog exceeded those of its gekkonid competitors by several orders of magnitude, the actual length of the season is similar in southern Florida. The Indo-Pacific gecko produces no more than two eggs (7.0–10.2 mm) at a time (Voss 1975; Meshaka 1994b, 2000), but reproduction in this all-female species (Kluge and Eckhardt 1969) is continuous in southern Florida, including the Everglades, and at least three clutches are possible annually (Meshaka 1994b). I also collected females with shelled eggs throughout the year in the region from Palmdale to Lake Placid, Florida. The wood slave reproduces continuously in southern Florida, including the Everglades, and produces at least four clutches annually (Meshaka et al. 1993; Meshaka 2000).

Table 5.18. Egg-laying activity of the Cuban treefrog from a residential swimming pool in Key West in 1991 and 1993.

Month	1991 No. breeding nights	1991 Min. air temp.	1991 Rainfall	1993 No. breeding nights	1993 Min. air temp.	1993 Rainfall	1945–1986 Min. air temp	1945–1986 Rainfall
Jan	0	21.0	5.7	0	21.2	0.2	18.4	4.4
Feb	0	19.9	0.7	0	21.5	0.8	18.7	4.9
Mar	0	21.4	7.4	0	19.3	3.6	21.0	3.3
Apr	0	24.6	3.7	0	20.4	4.5	23.2	3.8
May	1	25.4	20.5	1	23.9	11.2	24.8	8.2
Jun	3	25.9	21.4	0	26.4	4.3	26.0	12.8
Jul	0	26.9	5.6	0	27.2	1.1	26.9	9.4
Aug	3	26.6	5.7	3	26.7	9.7	26.7	12.2
Sep	3	25.9	13.7	7	26.2	14.6	26.1	16.5
Oct	0	24.5	18.1	4	24.5	15.3	24.5	12.1
Nov	0	21.6	0.3	0	22.9	0.6	22.1	12.1
Dec	0	20.2	1.8	0	18.7	5.6	19.5	4.4

The 41-year average (1945–1986) for average monthly thermal low (°C) and monthly total volume of rainfall (cm) for Key West were provided by the Key West Public Library.

Sex ratios

Cuban treefrog tadpoles have yet to be reared to sexual maturity to answer the question, what is the sex ratio of this species as individuals enter the adult population? However, the sex ratio (M:F) of 1,802 adults captured in a two-year period from the park was even (0.82). The sex ratio, although even over time, differed between places during the breeding season.

For that reason, I believe that males resided at breeding sites in the wet season for longer periods of time than females. For example, during three major road crossings (21 May 1991, 10 June 1992, 3 September 1992) and two breeding aggregations (24 March 1992, 10 June 1992), I collected 152 males and 28 females. When I removed these individuals, I calculated a sex ratio of 0.69. This value was significantly biased ($\chi^2_{df = 2}$ = 42.0, $P < 0.00$) to resident females of nonbreeding sites. Despite differential use of the habitat, at least as many females as males existed in the adult population, which provided half the population with the opportunity to lay eggs and return to nonbreeding, feeding sites.

Collections of green treefrogs, squirrel treefrogs, and wood slaves also revealed even sex ratios. Like the wood slaves, other successful colonizing species of amphibians and reptiles in Florida exhibit an even sex ratio, not handicapped by a sex ratio that favors males. For example, an annual sample I made of marine toads in Lake Placid, Florida, was evenly distributed between the sexes. The same was true of a population of Mediterranean geckos, also from Lake Placid (Meshaka 1995), and during three years of marking and recapturing knight anoles in Homestead (Meshaka, unpubl. data), my capture rates were equal for both sexes.

Reproduction-related movements

For both years of the study in the park, April–October was the period of greatest reproductive activity for the Cuban treefrog. Within this period, reproduction-related movements were pronounced and predictable in their association with rainfall. For instance, the third week of May 1991 and the first week of June 1992 marked the first major storms of the summer rainy season (table 5.1). The intensity of the May rains of 1991 was striking. Weather conditions on the evening of 20 May 1991 were windy, cool (23.0 °C), and rainy (9.9 cm). Choruses were deafening as adults crossed Long Pine Key Road en masse. Despite frequent visits to many sites, nothing of this magnitude was seen again until June 1992.

During the first breeding event of the season, a similar but less intense migration was observed, with 10.8 cm of rain, throughout the night hours of 7 June 1992. Monthly volume of rainfall was closely associated with seasonal movement across both Long Pine Key Road (r = 0.90, P < 0.000) and Main Park Road (r = 0.78, P < 0.003). Conditions associated with movements across roads (table 5.12) were significantly warmer ($\chi^2_{df = 8}$ = 129.09, P < 0.000) and wetter ($\chi^2_{df = 6}$ = 31.40, P < 0.000) with respect to volume of rainfall than those of nocturnal calling. However, movements so closely associated with reproductive activity occurred under equally high rainfall levels as oviposition.

Hurricane-related response in reproduction

Obviously, the Cuban treefrog was a true rain frog, but unlike nearly all of Florida's native herpetofauna, it also evolved in the presence of hurricanes. Therefore, in light of its dependence on rainfall for all aspects of reproductive activities, its positive reproductive response to Hurricane Andrew (Meshaka 1993) should not be surprising. In fact, this species not only tolerated hurricanes but also took advantage of the corresponding weather conditions for reproduction, also the case in the park.

A greater breeding event than that of May 1991 apparently took place in September 1992, immediately after Hurricane Andrew (23–24 August 1992). On 20 August 1992, activity of this species and numbers of gravid females were as low as the August visit of the previous year. On 3 September 1992, after approximately 15 cm of rain from Hurricane Andrew, I collected a large series of gravid females from the park. This was interesting because gravid females were also more numerous in the months following Hurricane Andrew than they were the year before despite less rainfall.

Females responded to the disturbance not only with a readiness to reproduce, but also with a body-size component. I found that from my first monthly collections in November 1990 up until one week before Hurricane Andrew struck southern Florida two years later, the mean body size of gravid individuals was significantly larger than nongravid counterparts (table 5.19). Generally larger, presumably older, females contributed most to reproduction in other populations (tables 5.20, 5.21). The same was not true for a sample of *O. dominicencis*. However, immediately after Hurricane Andrew (September–November 1992), the mean body size of gravid females was similar to that of nongravid females. That is to say, no longer were large females carrying the burden of reproduction. Gravid

Table 5.19. Body sizes (mm SVL) of gravid and nongravid female Cuban treefrogs from the southern Everglades before Hurricane Andrew and immediately afterwards.

Period	Gravid	Nongravid	Significance
Before Andrew	70.0 ± 10.1; 47.1–94.0; 136*	62.9 ± 10.5; 44.5–93.8; 695	$T_{df = 829} = -7.25$, $P < 0.000$
After Andrew	64.7 ± 8.0; 52.0–82.0; 45	65.8 ± 9.5; 44.5–91.4; 111	N.S.

N.S. statistically not significant ($P > 0.05$).
* one large female could not be measured.

females collected after the hurricane were significantly smaller ($t_{df = 55} = 3.57$, $P < 0.0006$) in body size than those collected immediately before the hurricane, and nongravid females collected after the hurricane were larger ($t_{df = 806} = -2.11$, $P < 0.04$) than they had been before the hurricane (table 5.19).

To better understand the problem, I plotted the number of large and small gravid females examined during the six periods January–April, May–August, and September–December 1991 and 1992 (table 5.22). During a normal year, such as year 1 (November 1990–October 1991),

Table 5.20. Statistical comparisons between fertile and sexually quiescent males and gravid and nongravid females of the Cuban treefrog and *Osteopilus dominicensis*.

Location	Males	Females
Cuban treefrog		
Southern Everglades	$F = 1.41$, $T_{df = 422} = -8.44$	
Cuba	$F = 2.57$, $T_{df = 31} = -2.59$	$T_{df = 178} = -4.10$
Cayman Islands	N.S.	N.S.
Bahamas	N.S.	N.S.
Florida		
Lower Florida Keys	N.S.	N.S.
Palmdale	$T_{df = 49} = 3.96$	$T_{df = 75} = -5.27$
Lake Placid	N.S.	$T_{df = 30} = -210$
Okeechobee	$T_{df = 123} = 7.42$	$F = 2.38$, $T_{df = 177} = -4.78$
Tampa	$T_{df = 39} = -3.80$	$F = 1.97$, $T_{df = 65} = -5.00$
O. dominicensis	$F = 6.2$, $Z = -1.38$, $P < 0.04$	N.S.

$P < 0.000$ unless otherwise stated.
N.S. statistically not significant ($P > 0.05$).

Table 5.21. Body length in mm as snout-vent length (SVL) for the Cuban treefrog and its competitors.

Location	Male	Female	Difference
Cuban treefrog			
Everglades National Park			
All	46.1 ± 5.1; 28.9–59.8; 814	64.2 ± 10.6; 44.5–99.0; 987	F = 4.58, T$_{df=1,455}$ = −47.64
Fertile/gravid	47.3 ± 4.4; 35.8–59.8; 560		
Sexually quiescent/not gravid	44.1 ± 5.3; 28.6–56.5; 254		
Amplectant	45.1 ± 2.8; 40.5–49.7; 10	67.1 ± 8.9; 47.0–80.8; 10	
Cuba			
All	47.4 ± 7.8; 27.0–83.0; 180	71.8 ± 13.4; 44.1–122.0; 212	F = 2.96, T$_{df=348}$ = 22.4
Fertile/gravid	48.3 ± 6.8; 27.4–65.0; 152	78.4 ± 12.1; 59.0–122.0; 64	
Sexually quiescent/not gravid	42.8 ± 10.7; 27.0–83.0; 28	68.9 ± 10.9; 44.1–110.0; 148	
Cayman Islands			
All	53.2 ± 7.0; 38.5–89.0; 64	75.6 ± 11.4; 47.1–119.0; 118	
Fertile/gravid	53.2 ± 6.6; 38.5–89.0; 56	77.5 ± 8.6; 56.3–91.6; 40	
Sexually quiescent/not gravid	53.0 ± 9.1; 45.4–74.9; 8	74.6 ± 12.5; 47.1–119.0; 78	
Bahamas			
All	44.0 ± 6.3; 29.0–58.0; 102	65.8 ± 1.6; 44.6–83.8; 57	F = 1.87, T$_{df=90}$ = 13.41
Fertile/gravid	44.5 ± 4.9; 37.4–58.0; 50	64.6 ± 4.7; 58.0–73.6; 8	
Sexually quiescent/not gravid	43.5 ± 7.4; 29.0–57.0; 52	61.1 ± 8.9; 44.6–83.8; 49	
Lower Florida Keys			
All	52.9 ± 3.4; 47.0–58.5; 20	71.3 ± 5.1; 62.1–80.5; 33	F = 2.14, T$_{df=50}$ = −15.4
Palmdale, Florida			
All	46.9 ± 5.1; 34.4–56.6; 51	57.3 ± 7.6; 45.0–81.0; 77	F = −2.18, T$_{df=126}$ = 9.21
Fertile/gravid	49.9 ± 3.7; 41.0–56.6; 21	66.0 ± 6.8; 56.9–81.0; 13	
Sexually quiescent/not gravid	44.8 ± 4.9; 34.4–55.9; 30	55.5 ± 6.4; 45.0–68.8; 64	
Lake Placid, Florida			
All	47.9 ± 9.6; 34.4–85.0; 24	67.3 ± 12.5; 50.4–122.0; 36	T$_{df=58}$ = 6.31
Fertile/gravid	51.3 ± 14.5; 41.2–85.0; 7	72.6 ± 6.1; 64.2–85.9; 9	
Sexually quiescent/not gravid	46.5 ± 6.1; 34.4–62.5; 17	65.5 ± 13.6; 50.4–72.2; 27	

Okeechobee, Florida			
All	46.6 ± 5.8; 34.4–58.8; 114	62.7 ± 9.3; 44.8–96.6; 180	$F = 2.47$, $T_{df=238} = 18.1$
Fertile/gravid	49.3 ± 4.4; 37.0–58.8; 68	66.1 ± 6.7; 50.5–88.4; 74	
Sexually quiescent/not gravid	42.5 ± 5.2; 34.4–54.0; 46	60.4 ± 10.2; 44.8–96.6; 106	
Tampa, Florida			
All	47.7 ± 5.2; 35.9–59.0; 41	63.3 ± 8.6; 45.0–86.0; 87	$F = 2.75$, $T_{df=118} = -12.7$
Fertile/gravid	49.3 ± 4.2; 42.0–59.9; 29	69.0 ± 6.0; 57.5–82.0; 27	
Sexually quiescent/not gravid	43.3 ± 5.1; 35.9–54.0; 12	60.9 ± 8.5; 45.0–86.0; 60	
Osteopilus dominicensis			
All	57.3 ± 7.5; 34.0–80.0; 91	80.9 ± 11.1; 48.0–100.0; 46	$F = 2.20$, $T_{df=67} = -12.4$
Fertile/ gravid	58.0 ± 6.1; 42.0–70.0; 83	81.8 ± 8.8; 62.0–100.0; 30	
Sexually quiescent/not gravid	50.5 ± 14.3; 34.0–80.0; 8	77.8 ± 15.2; 48.0–100.0; 16	
Green treefrog			
Everglades National Park			
All	36.4 ± 4.9; 28.0–49.0; 63	43.7 ± 5.5; 32–55; 100	$T_{df=161} = -8.62$
Squirrel treefrog			
Everglades National Park			
All	25.8 ± 3.0; 21.5–34.0; 55	25.9 ± 3.2; 20.0–37.0; 82	N.S.
Indo-Pacific gecko			
ENP			
All		49.0–61.3	
Wood slave			
ENP			
All	58.7 ± 5.1; 52.0–66.0; 9	58.5 ± 5.0; 47.4–67.0; 27	N.S.

Mean value followed by standard deviation, range of values, and sample size. P < 0.000 unless stated as not significant (N.S.).

Table 5.22. Numbers of large (70.0 + mm SVL) and small (≤ 69.9 mm SVL) gravid females of the Cuban treefrog collected in the southern Everglades.

Month	Large I	Small I	Large II	Small II	Total
Jan–Apr	2	1	13	4	20
May–Aug	16	29	21	35	101
Sep–Dec	15	1	9	36	61
Total	33	31	43	75	182

I. November 1990–October 1991.
II. November 1991–November 1992.

both large and small females bred infrequently during January–April. However, large gravid females were evenly distributed during May–August and September–December, but small gravid females were detected nearly exclusively during May–August, meaning that in a normal year small females breed most often in the summer, whereas breeding readiness is more evenly distributed among large females.

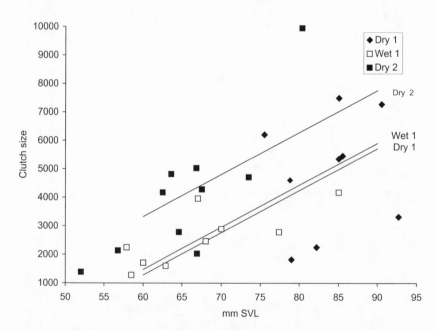

Figure 5.5. Relationship of clutch size to snout-vent length (mm SVL) of 28 Cuban treefrogs from the southern Everglades during October 1991–March 1992 (Dry 1), May 1992 (Wet 1), and October 1992 (Dry 2) with corresponding regression lines adjusted for body size.

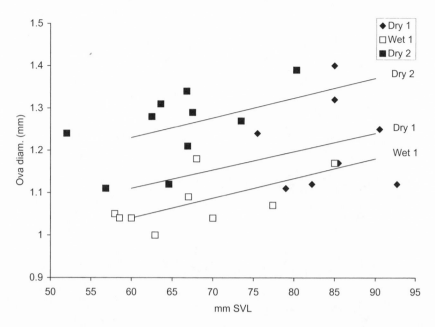

Figure 5.6. Relationship of ova diameter (mm) with snout-vent length (mm SVL) of 28 Cuban treefrogs from the southern Everglades during October 1991–March 1992 (Dry 1), May 1992 (Wet 1), and October 1992 (Dry 2) with corresponding regression lines adjusted for body size.

Year 2 (November 1991–November 1992) provided the test because it was interrupted by the particularly strong hurricane in the summer period. During that year, large females were gravid through the winter and, like the previous year, during the May–August period. Uncharacteristically, however, numbers of large gravid females dropped immediately after the hurricane. The opposite was true for small females. For both years, the distribution of small gravid females was similar during January–April and May–August. However, in September–December 1992, which coincided with the hurricane, small females experienced an uncharacteristic spike in the numbers of gravid individuals, and this hurricane-related response in reproduction was evident in small females much more so than in their larger counterparts (table 5.22).

The hurricane affected not only the body size distribution of breeding females but the clutch characteristics as well (figs. 5.5 and 5.6, tables 5.23 and 5.24). With the effect of body size removed, clutch size and ova diameter measured prior to Hurricane Andrew in the dry season (October 1991–March 1992) and in the following wet season (May 1992) were

Table 5.23. Test of between subject effects in the comparison of clutch size and egg size of the Cuban treefrog among three different time periods in the southern Everglades.

Source	Dependent Variable	Type III Sum of Squares	df	Mean Square	F	Sig.
Corrected Model	Clutch size	55941725.924[b]	3	18647241.975	6.780	.002
	Egg size	.195[c]	3	6.502E-02	9.877	.000
Intercept	Clutch size	12799369.194	1	12799369.194	4.654	.042
	Egg size	.201	1	.201	30.475	.000
SVL	Clutch size	31629689.616	1	31629689.616	11.500	.003
	Egg size	2.905E-02	1	2.905E-02	4.413	.047
Time Period	Clutch size	18319355.549	2	9159677.774	3.330	.054
	Egg size	.168	2	8.399E-02	12.759	.000
Error	Clutch size	63258477.484	23	2750368.586		
	Egg size	.151	23	6.583E-03		
Total	Clutch size	516533084.0	27			
	Egg size	38.201	27			
Corrected Total	Clutch size	119200203.4	26			
	Egg size	.346	26			

[a] Computed using alpha = 0.05

[b] R Squared = .469 (Adjusted R Squared = .400)

[c] R Squared = .563 (Adjusted R Squared = .506)

Table 5.24. Parameter estimates in the comparison of clutch size and egg size of the Cuban treefrog among three different time periods in the southern Everglades.

Dependent Variable	Parameter	B	Std. Error	t	Sig.	95% Confidence Interval	
						Lower Bound	Upper Bound
Clutch size	Intercept	-5553.870	2903.413	-1.913	.068	-11560.038	452.298
	SVL	147.961	46.631	3.391	.003	57.704	238.219
	[Dry Period 1]	-2042.517	1142.038	-1.788	.087	-4405.003	319.970
	[Wet Period 1]	-1852.369	766.782	-2.416	.024	-3438.578	-266.159
	[Dry Period 2]	0[b]	.	.	.	.	.
Egg size	Intercept	.963	.283	2.743	.006	.669	1.256
	SVL	4.588E-03	.004	1.026	.306	6.828E-05	8.900E-02
	[Dry Period 1]	-.125	.191	-1.098	.273	-.240	-9.254E-03
	[Wet Period 1]	-.189	.299	3.850	.000	-.267	-.112
	[Dry Period 2]	0[b]	.	.	.	.	.

[b] This parameter is set to zero because it is redundant.

equally small. Clutches measured at the end of the wet season (October 1992), two months after Hurricane Andrew, were significantly larger in number of eggs and in ova diameter than either previous sample. Not only, then, did small females replace large females in breeding after the hurricane, but per unit body size they produced larger clutches of larger eggs. Small-bodied males were afforded no hurricane-related advantage to reproduction; no such body-size component associated with the hurricane occurred in males, the largest of which were often the most likely to be fertile (tables 5.20, 5.21).

Why would this be? Why would large females that usually contributed most to breeding suddenly be replaced by smaller females after a hurricane? A body-size component to early breeding, although not previously known in the Cuban treefrog, has been documented in other species. Downhower (1976) observed that among sparrows, the small females were ready to reproduce before their larger counterparts. This phenomenon was explained simply by energetic demands; energetic needs of small females were less than those of large females, and therefore easier to meet for reproduction. Perhaps small female Cuban treefrogs generally lay their eggs in the summer period, as disclosed in year 1, and put their subsequent energy into growth for reproduction the following year. Upon achieving a large body size, females distribute clutch production throughout the year, especially during the summer through early winter when conditions are very suitable for egg laying. Because of extended breeding activity and large body size, large females consequently outcompete small females for annual number of clutches and eggs. Relevant to Downhower's (1976) hypothesis is that although females of all size-classes exploited a physical disturbance and did so with extraordinarily large clutch sizes, small females, because of their fewer energetic needs, more rapidly mobilized energy (fat or direct food intake) into clutch production than females. The result was a body-size component to disturbance-related reproduction that favored small females, momentarily allowing them to outcompete what were usually more fecund large females.

6

Larval Development and Postmetamorphic Growth

Eggs and tadpoles

Once laid, the eggs, and subsequently the tadpoles, of the Cuban treefrog were on their own. In the southern Everglades, its eggs are deposited in a thin surface film as partial clutches in parcels generally of 200 to 300 eggs (Duellman and Schwartz 1958; Meshaka 1993; this study), seldom exceeding 1,000 eggs. Hard rain causes clutches to sink. The egg masses are very sticky through at least the first fifteen hours of development and are less sticky during hatching, generally within thirty hours of oviposition (Schwartz 1952; Meshaka 1993).

The stickiness may serve to protect the eggs from predators, including conspecifics. Several lines of evidence suggest that the phenomenon of cannibalism may well be strong enough to select for sticky eggs. For example, I rarely found Cuban treefrog eggs at sites containing conspecific tadpoles that were more than a few days old and big enough to damage eggs. At closed sites, no more than one cohort of tadpoles was ever observed at one time, and, in captivity, Cuban treefrog tadpoles voraciously ate freshly laid and developing eggs.

I never examined the palatability of native anuran eggs to Cuban treefrog tadpoles. Of particular interest were the species most often found in the shallow still water favored by the Cuban treefrog. In the southern Everglades, the likeliest candidates for egg predation by the Cuban treefrog were the Florida chorus frog (*Pseudacris nigrita verrucosa*), little grass frog (*P. ocularis*), the squirrel treefrog (*Hyla squirella*), and the eastern narrowmouth toad (*Gastrophryne carolinensis*). To a lesser extent, the southern toad (*Bufo terrestris*) and oak toad (*B. quercicus*) occasionally overlapped with the Cuban treefrog in their choice of oviposition sites, so their eggs were also potential prey.

Predicting where to find Cuban treefrog tadpoles was relatively easy. Three conditions are common to their presence. First, tadpoles were absent from sites with predaceous fish. Extensive and very shallow and grassy margins of permanent water inhabited by predaceous fish were occasional exceptions to this rule if the grassy margins could not be invaded by predaceous fish. Second, sites with mean summer afternoon temperatures below 30 °C were devoid, or nearly so, of tadpoles. Third, sites with recorded mean water depths of >45.0 cm were devoid of tadpoles. The last condition was likely in response to the negative association between water depth and water temperature (r =-0.71, $P < 0.005$; N = 14). In the park, summer larval sites of Long Pine Key that met these requirements were virtually unlimited.

Tadpoles were collected year round in some disturbed and most natural sites. Only the marsh and pond were devoid of tadpoles and adults. Tadpoles were found in Taylor Slough at Royal Palm Hammock; however, the breeding site was not typical of the conditions associated with a slough. Tadpoles were found in one very shallow artificial shore next to a concession building. The shallow water and thick aquatic vegetation effectively protected adults and tadpoles from predatory fish until late in the wet season when high water and fish in the depression precluded further use of this site for development. The depression created from a toppled strangler fig tree (*Ficus aurea*) during Hurricane Andrew provided another larval site at Taylor Slough with the same temporal limitations as the artificial shore. Tadpoles were observed throughout the year in one solution hole and were present at most of the fourteen sites during the June–October collecting period.

Elsewhere in Florida I observed Cuban treefrog tadpoles in sewers, cisterns, ruts in roads, swails, flooded fields, and culverts. In Cuba, tadpoles have been recorded from drains around buildings (Schwartz and Ogren 1956). In the Cayman Islands, I found tadpoles and adults in cisterns.

Larval growth

Larval growth was generally rapid. Field estimates of a three-to-four-week larval period were similar to larval periods under captive conditions. Tadpoles raised at a constant 25.0 °C or within 24.5–34.0 °C transformed in 27 days at 15.5 ± 0.8 mm SVL and 14.8 ± 0.9 mm SVL, respectively (Meshaka 1993). In even hotter water with sufficient food, natural developmental times of less than three weeks seem probable.

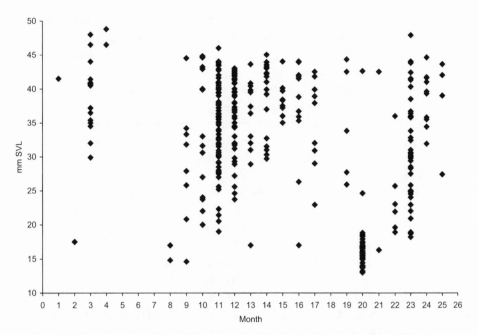

Figure 6.1. Snout-vent lengths (mm SVL) of 349 juvenile Cuban treefrogs collected during November 1990 (1)–November 1992 (25) in the southern Everglades.

Tadpoles were collected from the field in water that ranged 10.0–41.0 °C, and eggs were laid throughout the year. Consequently, larval time of the Cuban treefrog varied greatly in the other direction. For example, in 1997 at my residence in Homestead, calling began during the second week in April. Spawning and hatching took place during the last week of April in a birdbath with little algal growth, and tadpoles required three months to transform. Immediately after the first cohort transformed in early August, a second spawn was laid in what was by then a hotter and more eutrophic system. Tadpoles of that cohort transformed within 30 days of oviposition. A few days after metamorphosis of that cohort, a third spawn deposited in early September transformed by the third week of October. The last calling and spawning of the season took place in the swimming pool during the third week of October. Finally, some of those tadpoles that were moved to a bucket did not transform until the end of the following March. I noticed the apparent "overwintering" in a shaded solution hole in the park and in artificial ponds in Miami.

Having encountered a wide range of temperatures, Cuban treefrog tadpoles behaved accordingly. Tadpoles ventured into shallow open regions from dusk until dawn and throughout overcast days and also foraged openly in low light conditions. On cold but sunny days, tadpoles in deep pools congregated in tight groups to bask at the water's surface.

For both years of the study in the park, June–September was the interval during which the greatest number of metamorphic individuals was collected out of the water (fig. 6.1), and June–October 1991 was the interval of greatest dipnet captures of metamorphoslings. Using either measure, the highest numbers of metamorphic individuals overlapped the bimodal pulse of breeding activity during the summer rainy season. For example, on a building located 300 m from the May 1991 migration, I counted 35 metamorphic individuals on 19 June 1991, just one month after the migration. Three weeks after the June 1992 migration, I collected 19 recently transformed individuals (16.0 ± 1.5 mm SVL; range = 13.0–18.5) on a building at Royal Palm Hammock at 1:00 A.M. on 26 June 1992 and 26 more individuals from the same building (16.0 ± 1.4 mm SVL; range = 13.2–18.8) at 1:00 the following night.

Metamorphoslings were large, but similar to those of at least one site in the West Indies. During the third week in June 1994, I collected a series of metamorphoslings (15.3 ± 2.1 mm SVL; range = 15.0–18.5; N = 22) from a fountain at the Palacio de las Convenciones in Havana. Most of the specimens, including the largest individuals, had not yet absorbed their tails. These data revealed that Cuban treefrog metamorphoslings are large throughout the geographic range of the species.

Postmetamorphic growth and maturity

The Everglades was just rebounding from a two-year drought when I began my study during late 1990. My collection of 2,151 individuals over two years comprised 349 juveniles, which represented 16.2 percent of a rapidly recruiting population. Such rapid recruitment, remarkable though it was, was no surprise once I learned just how fast this species matured.

The smallest metamorphoslings (12.2 ± 1.8 mm SVL; range = 10.5–16.0; N = 17) were on average 45 percent of the body size of a recently mature male (27 mm SVL). Using a conservative estimate of 4.0 mm of growth per month, as gleaned from the scattergram (fig. 6.1), males, needing only barely to double in body size from metamorphosis, matured within three months of transformation. Although growth rates probably differed between wet and dry seasons, growth rates in mature males appeared to slow down to approximately 3.0 mm per month upon maturity (fig. 6.2). This being the case, average body size of approximately 46 mm

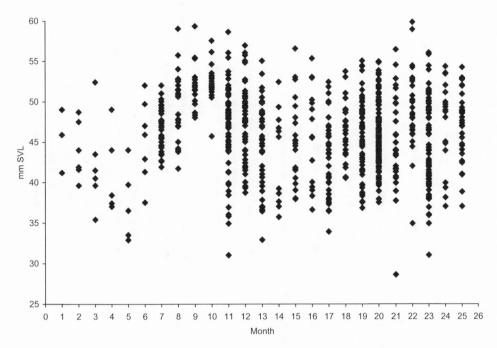

Figure 6.2. Snout-vent lengths (mm SVL) of 814 male Cuban treefrogs collected during November 1990 (1)–November 1992 (25) in the southern Everglades.

SVL (table 5.21) was reached at nine months after transformation, and the largest males (55–60 mm SVL) were dead at the end of their first year of life or very shortly thereafter.

Maturity in Everglades females, although a little slower than in males, was also rapid. Metamorphoslings were on average 27 percent the body size of a recently mature female (45 mm SVL). Using the same growth rate of 4.0 mm per month, I estimated sexual maturity in females to be attained at seven or eight months after transformation (fig. 6.1), when males of that cohort had reached their average body size and were beginning to die. After sexual maturity, growth rates remained steady until females reached their mean body size of approximately 65 mm SVL (table 5.21) at the end of their first year of life (fig. 6.3), when the last of their male cohorts was dead. Subsequent growth rates decreased to approximately 3.0 mm per month until females were at about 80 mm SVL, at which time growth slowed to 0.5–2.3 mm per month. This being the case, the largest females probably died as they approached three years of life from transformation.

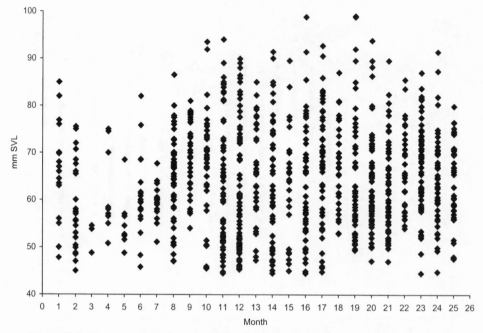

Figure 6.3. Snout-vent lengths (mm SVL) of 987 female Cuban treefrogs collected during November 1990 (1)–November 1992 (25) in the southern Everglades.

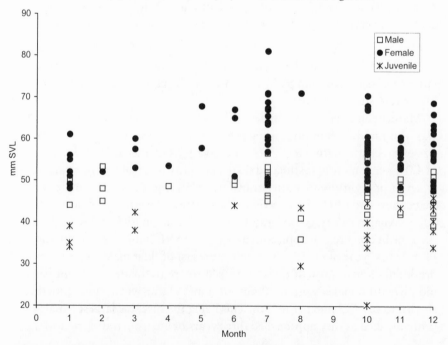

Figure 6.4. Snout-vent lengths (mm SVL) of 51 male, 77 female, and 23 juvenile Cuban treefrogs collected during March 1993–December 1994 in Palmdale, Florida.

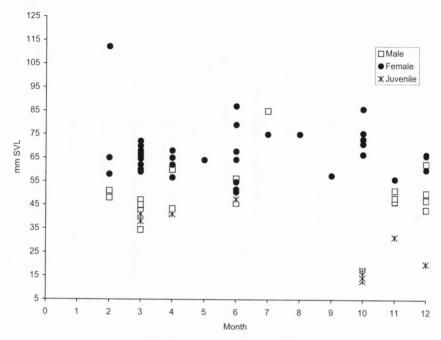

Figure 6.5. Snout-vent lengths (mm SVL) of 24 male, 36 female, and 18 juvenile Cuban treefrogs collected during February 1993–April 1995 in Lake Placid, Florida.

A slight but noticeable modification to the pattern of rapid growth and short lifespan was detected in Florida populations of Cuban treefrogs located north of the southern Everglades (figs. 6.4–6.7). In Palmdale, Lake Placid, Okeechobee, and Tampa, males were smaller than females (table 5.21), and juvenile growth rate was approximately 3.5 mm per month. Growth patterns of males and females were especially evident in the scattergrams from Okeechobee (fig. 6.6) and Tampa (fig. 6.7). Males of those regions matured in about four months and grew approximately 2.2 mm per month until they achieved their mean body size (table 5.21) about seven or eight months later, a little later than their southern counterparts. At this time, they were about one year of age since transformation and many began to die. Growth rates of the few remaining larger males slowed down to 0.7–1.1 mm per month, extending their lives to nearly two years.

Females matured in eight or nine months after transformation and reached their mean body size five months later at approximately 4.0 mm per month. Growth rates of larger females slowed to 2.0–3.0 mm per

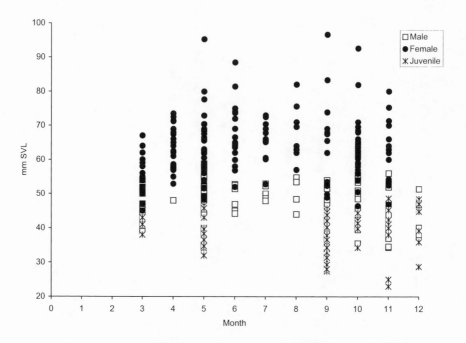

Figure 6.6. Snout-vent lengths (mm SVL) of 114 male, 180 female, and 72 juvenile Cuban treefrogs collected during November 1991–March 1995 in Okeechobee, Florida.

month. Like those of the southern Everglades, very few females farther north were alive after two years of postmetamorphic life.

Postmetamorphic growth and maturity of Cuban populations were more similar to the patterns in the southern Everglades than to northern populations. Minimum body size at sexual maturity was smaller in males (27 mm SVL) than in females (44 mm SVL) from Cuba (table 5.21; figs. 6.8, 6.9). Based on minimum size at maturity and from a body size scattergram (figs. 6.8–6.10), males were mature in two to three months after transformation, having grown approximately 5.0 mm per month. Average body size of adult males was achieved at seven to eight months after transformation, with growth of 4.1 mm per month postmetamorphosis. When average body size was reached, growth slowed to 2.5 mm per month; twelve to thirteen months after transformation, males reached maximum adult size and began to die.

At 5.0 mm per month, females reached sexual maturity at six or seven months after transformation. However, age of females at mean body size at maturity was difficult to ascertain from the graph (fig. 6.9).

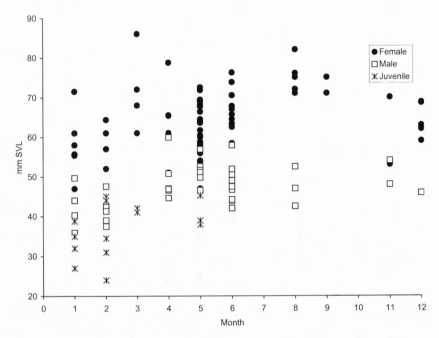

Figure 6.7. Snout-vent lengths (mm SVL) of 41 male, 87 female, and 15 juvenile Cuban treefrogs collected during November 1992–November 1997 in Tampa, Florida. Specimens available from the University of South Florida Vertebrate Collection were collected as early as 1973.

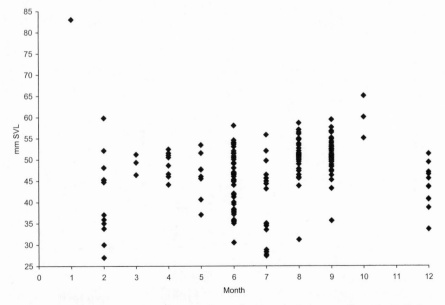

Figure 6.8. Snout-vent lengths (mm SVL) of 180 male Cuban treefrogs from Cuba.

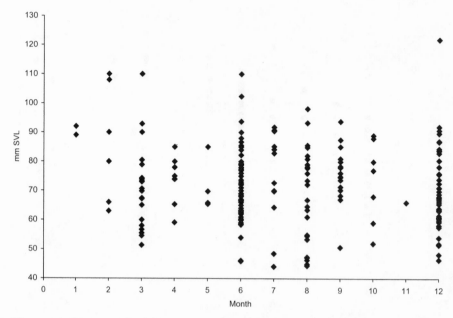

Figure 6.9. Snout-vent lengths (mm SVL) of 212 female Cuban treefrogs from Cuba.

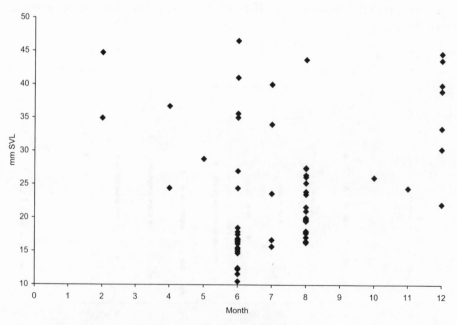

Figure 6.10. Snout-vent lengths (mm SVL) of 71 juvenile Cuban treefrogs from Cuba.

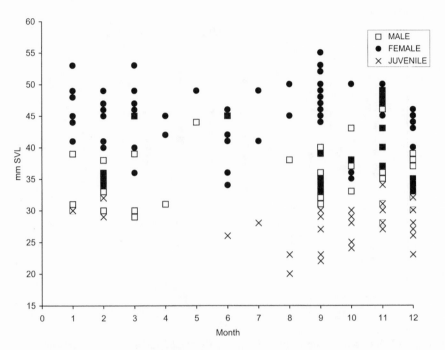

Figure 6.11. Snout-vent lengths (mm SVL) of 63 male, 100 female, and 39 juvenile green treefrogs collected during November 1990–November 1992 in Everglades National Park.

Among its native hylid competitors, sexual maturity was reached by both sexes at similarly small body sizes and within one year (table 5.2; figs. 6.11, 6.12). The same was true for the wood slave, *Hemidactylus mabouia* (table 5.21; fig. 6.13; Meshaka et al. 1993; Meshaka 2000). The all-female Indo-Pacific gecko (*H. garnotii*) was mature at a body size (49.2 mm SVL) similar to that of the wood slave and also matured in one year (Meshaka 1994b, 2000).

Other successful colonizers in Florida also mature within the first year of life. The list of species includes the knight anole (*Anolis equestris equestris*), the brown anole (*A. sagrei*), and the bark anole (*A. distichus*) (King 1966). In Panama, the marine toad (*Bufo marinus*) also matures within one year (Zug and Zug 1979).

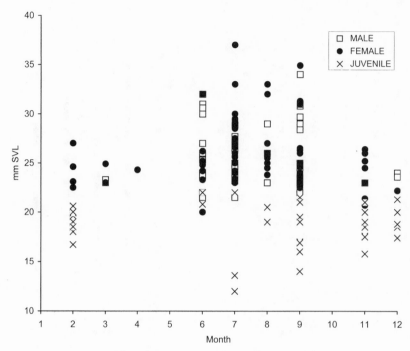

Figure 6.12. Snout-vent lengths (mm SVL) of 55 male, 82 female, and 47 juvenile squirrel treefrogs collected during November 1990–November 1992 in Everglades National Park.

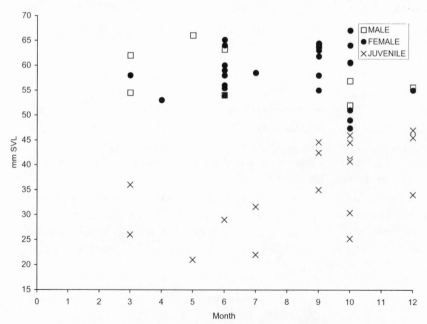

Figure 6.13. Snout-vent lengths (mm SVL) of 9 male, 27 female, and 19 juvenile wood slaves collected during November 1991–November 1998 in Everglades National Park.

7

Seasonal and Nightly Activity

Seasonal activity

The southern Everglades is a rain-driven system punctuated by distinct wet and dry seasons. Breeding amplitudes were greatest during the wet season, but what was this species doing during the rest of the year? In the park, the Cuban treefrog was active throughout the year (table 7.1), especially during the wet season (table 7.2). The late summer flush of juveniles (fig. 6.1) could be responsible for the absence of any significant relationship ($r = 0.19$, $P < 0.56$) between monthly abundance and rainfall.

I did not systematically collect Cuban treefrogs in other areas of Florida but my collecting visits were frequent and more organized than opportunistic. The seasonal difference in the numbers of Cuban treefrogs collected from Florida sites other than the park I believe to be an accurate reflection of a more defined seasonality to this species in northern (colder) and insular (drier) populations, similar to their breeding activities.

Activity of Cuban populations, highly seasonal, is more pronounced in the wet season months (Schwartz and Henderson 1991), in association with most breeding activities (table 5.7). This observation is supported in museum records of many large summer collections, as compared to few dry season collections, which contained only a few individuals (figs. 6.8–6.10). In this connection, I captured 67 individuals in only a few days during my June 1993 visit to Cuba; at that time Cuban treefrogs were seemingly everywhere. The same was true for the Bahamas. I do not have firsthand field-collected data from the dry season; however, my impression of pronounced activity of this species during the wet season was corroborated by accounts of local residents.

Among native competitors, the green treefrog (*Hyla cinerea*) was active throughout the year (table 7.1) but most abundant in the dry season (table 7.2). Seasonal abundance at its most populated site was greater during the

Table 7.1. Relative abundance of the Cuban treefrog on the Daniel Beard Center, the green treefrog at Pahayokee, and the squirrel treefrog at Pahayokee.

Month	Cuban treefrog	Green treefrog	Squirrel treefrog	Rainfall	
				Daniel Beard Center	Pahayokee
Aug	38	0	7	11.2	13.8
Sep	42	4	13	39.5	16.8
Oct	79	6	21	13.7	20.0
Nov	29	15	7	0.6	1.8
Dec	19	11	51	2.2	4.0
Jan-1992	19	14	27	3.0	2.7
Feb	3	13	60	3.7	3.2
Mar	21	2	7	4.8	6.4
Apr	8	1	3	6.1	6.9
May	10	1	1	1.8	6.2
Jun	16	0	0	53.8	5.5
Jul	23	1	1	12.6	5.1

Monthly totals of rainfall (cm) are presented for both sites.

Table 7.2. Statistical comparisons of seasonal activity in five species of amphibians and reptiles in Everglades National Park.

Species	Season		Significance
	Wet	Dry	
Cuban treefrog			
Daniel Beard Center[1]	32.7 ± 24.9; 10–79	16.5 ± 8.5; 1–29	$Z = 1.47, P < 0.04$
Green treefrog			
Pahayokee[1]	1.8 ± 2.4; 0–6	9.3 ± 4.7; 1–15	$Z = -2.35, P < 0.009$
Squirrel treefrog			
Pahayokee[1]	5.8 ± 8.6; 0–21	25.8 ± 22.0; 3–60	$Z = -1.76, P < 0.04$
Indo-Pacific gecko			
Fish Hut[1]	10.8 ± 2.9; 6–14*	9.3 ± 2.9; 7–15	N.S.
Fish Hut[2]	5.5 ± 4.1; 0–11	2.3 ± 1.8; 0–5	$Z = 1.58, P < 0.03$
Wood slave			
Fish Hut[2]	46.5 ± 9.7; 36–64	27.8 ± 11.2; 5–42	$Z = 1.64, P < 0.05$

1 = September 1991–August 1992. 2 = July 1995–June 1996. N.S = $P > 0.05$. * = Five months. Significance values are one-tailed.

dry season than during the wet season, perhaps because of the fall appearance of juveniles and the seasonal occupation of breeding sites by males. The same was true of the squirrel treefrog, *H. squirella* (tables 7.1, 7.2).

Both the Indo-Pacific gecko (*Hemidactylus garnotii*) and wood slave (*H. mabouia*) are active throughout the year (Meshaka 1994b, 2000). Their abundances in the park were higher in the wet season than during the dry season (table 7.2). The apparent absence of a seasonal component to the activity of the Indo-Pacific gecko in 1991 (table 7.2) may have been attributable to the lack of a full season of data collection in the wet season.

Without exception, all 39 exotic species of amphibians and reptiles established in Florida are active throughout the year, even if seasonal in their activity (Meshaka et al. 2001). Among the species studied at any length, two Cuban species, the knight anole (*Anolis equestris equestris*) and the greenhouse frog (*Eleutherodactylus planirostris planirostris*), and the marine toad (*Bufo marinus*), all tropical species, are strongly seasonal in activity.

Nightly activity

Put simply, the best time to expect to see Cuban treefrogs out and about in the southern Everglades was on humid, warm nights, when the relative humidity was in the 90s and the air temperature in the mid 20s °C (table 5.12). Looking at the range of physical conditions associated with nightly activity, I found that more so even than temperature, humidity was of primary importance: the Cuban treefrog depended on conditions approaching at least 90 percent RH to venture from its retreats. In light of its generally poor water economy (Meshaka 1996b) and reliance on co-ossification and phragmosis to retain water (Siebert et al. 1974), it made sense to see individuals resting flat on exposed surfaces on wet but cold nights.

As important as warmth and humidity were for general activity, their importance was even greater for calling activity, but within narrower ranges. Calling occurred under a narrower and higher range of air temperature, rainfall, and relative humidity (tables 5.11, 5.12, 7.3) than general activity. Consequently, geographic limitations imposed by weather constraints were more severe on the breeding activity of the Cuban treefrog than on its nightly activity.

I was surprised by the extent to which buildings conferred a positive effect on the activity of this species. In all of my visits to the park, I was never "skunked" when it came to finding Cuban treefrogs. Even on the coldest nights, I could always count on seeing at least something on build-

Table 7.3. Statistical comparisons of air temperature (°C), rainfall (cm), and relative humidity (%RH) associated with calling and nightly acitivty in the Cuban treefrog in natural sites of Everglades National Park.

	Nightly activity		
Parameter	Air temp.	Rainfall	Relative humidity
Calling	$X^2df = 22 = 57.87$	$X^2df = 6 = 70.16$	$X^2df = 35 = 64.81$

$P < 0.000$ unless otherwise stated.

ings. When nights were cold, and Cuban treefrogs were tucked away in their retreats in natural sites, I still saw individuals peeking out of wet drain pipes on buildings and out of the slats of the many "window shaker" air conditioning units, 52 in all, that ringed the DBC. When the night was very cold (9–12 °C), the high humidity and warm temperatures of the lighted LPK bathrooms quickly fogged my eyeglasses. With eyeglasses cleaned, I would see Cuban treefrogs out and about in hunting postures on beams and toilet bowl lids: effectively a greenhouse with frogs. For this striking reason, I separately analyzed air temperatures and activity for exterior-use-only buildings, interior/exterior-use buildings, and natural sites, and I found significant differences in the distribution of air temperatures associated with activity in the three habitat categories (table 5.12, 7.4). Cuban treefrogs in natural habitats were active in ambient temperatures warmer than those of exterior-use-only and interior/exterior-use buildings. Between building populations, activity occurred in cooler temperatures in interior/exterior-use buildings than in exterior-use-only buildings. Because Cuban treefrogs living in buildings were active when outside temperatures were too low to encourage activity on exterior-use buildings and in natural habitats, building-dwelling Cuban treefrogs, especially those of interior/exterior-use buildings, were provided with a thermal advantage over counterparts in nature.

Building versus nature comparisons in activity were not possible for the Cuban treefrog's competitors because either the competitors were rare on buildings (both treefrogs) or they were rare in nature (both geckos). However, respective comparisons disclosed that although the mean values of physical parameters for activity were similar among the five species in the park, the distributions of the air temperatures, rainfall, and humidity associated with nightly activity differed significantly between the Cuban

Table 7.4. Statistical comparisons of air temperatures associated with nightly activity of the Cuban treefrog in Everglades National Park from natural and building sites.

Habitat	Nature	Building
Building		Internal/external use
External use	$X^2df = 22 = 227.87$	$X^2df = 22 = 376.69$
Internal/external use	$X^2df = 22 = 161.85$	

P < 0.000 unless otherwise stated.

Table 7.5. Statistical comparison of air temperatures (°C), relative humidity (%RH), and rainfall (cm) associated with nightly activity of amphibians and reptiles in Everglades National Park.

Species	Cuban treefrog		
	Air temp.	Relative humidity	Rainfall
Green treefrog	$X^2df = 22 = 244.30$	$X^2df = 35 = 340.46$	$X^2df = 6 = 42.67$
Squirrel treefrog	$X^2df = 22 = 666.44$	$X^2df = 35 = 386.83$	$X^2df = 6 = 156.78$
Indo-Pacific gecko	$X^2df = 21 = 191.80$	$X^2df = 33 = 172.66$	$X^2df = 6 = 164.08$

P < 0.000 unless otherwise stated.

Table 7.6. Air temperatures (°C), relative humidity (%RH), and rainfall (cm) associated with activity of the wood slave and the Cuban treefrog on buildings at Flamingo in Everglades National Park during July 1995–June 1996.

Parameter	Wood slave	Cuban treefrog
Air temp.	25.1 ± 2.9; 16–30; 617	24.6 ± 2.9; 18–30; 39
Relative humidity	84.5 ± 10.8; 65–100; 645	86.7 ± 10.6; 65–100; 39
Rainfall	1.0 ± 2.9; 0–12.9; 606	1.6 ± 3.8; 0–12.9; 39

Means are followed by standard deviations, range of values, and sample size.
Data for the former species reprinted from Meshaka (2000).

treefrog and three of its competitors (table 7.5). The exception was the wood slave (table 7.6) at Flamingo—the Cuban treefrog was active in wetter conditions.

Diel patterns of activity

Cuban treefrogs in the southern Everglades were primarily but not exclusively nocturnal in their activity. Generally, individuals emerged at sunset from retreats and returned to retreats at first light. Exceptionally, amplectant pairs and solitary individuals were occasionally observed at breeding sites within 30 minutes after sunrise.

On days with very wet, humid, and overcast conditions, some individuals abandoned diurnal retreats and were by day found in resting posture in full exposure to the elements. In the midst of powerful low-pressure systems, males called intermittently through the day. On sunny days, large females were occasionally observed basking in broken sunlight near their retreats located several meters from the ground. Individuals of all body sizes would partially emerge from their retreats after a daytime rain shower, their eyes fully golden with pupils narrowed to slits. In Cuba, in the days following heavy rainstorms, I collected individuals by day in exposed situations and found that, as in Florida, large individuals bask in the sunlight (Schwartz and Henderson 1991).

The diel pattern of activity of its four competitors in the park was generally the same as that of the Cuban treefrog, and of the marine toad and greenhouse frog as well. With the exception of the yellow-headed gecko (*Gonatodes albogularis fuscus*), all of the introduced geckos of Florida are primarily nocturnal (Meshaka et al. 2001).

8

Habitat

Habitat affinity

In the park, the Cuban treefrog was found on buildings (figs. 4.12–4.18), in natural habitats (figs. 4.1–4.4, 4.6–4.10), and in disturbed habitats (figs. 4.5, 4.11; table 8.1), where it occupied the terrestrial-arboreal niche. Clearly, the best place to find this species was on buildings where its abundance was enhanced by, in descending order of importance, refuges (fig. 8.1), building size (fig. 8.2), and lights (fig. 8.3), and number of resident predator species (fig. 8.4). The importance of physical structure for the abundance of the Cuban treefrog was evident following structural changes of DBC and Iori buildings after Hurricane Andrew (figs. 4.12, 4.13). The difference between its abundance on the DBC during 1991–1992 and 1995–1996 was striking, but so were the structural changes associated with the latter period. Both buildings lost many of their lights and the large prey base attracted to those lights. When air conditioner units and awnings were removed, refuges associated with those structures were also lost. Consequently, a very real and sharp decrease in Cuban treefrog abundance occurred during 1995–1996 on the DBC ($t_{df = 12} = 3.59$, $P < 0.004$) and Iori building ($t_{df = 11} = 2.18$, $P < 0.05$).

Along eleven trails through natural and disturbed habitats, the Cuban treefrog was most common in forests (table 8.1). Its abundance along these trails, as on buildings, was best explained by the number of refuges (fig. 8.5), and by the dry season daytime relative humidity (fig. 8.6). Canopy cover and number of resident predator species did not significantly explain any of the variance in the abundance of the Cuban treefrog studied along trails.

Poor water economy (Meshaka 1996a), proclivity for refuges (Meshaka 1996a,b; this study), and a casqued head that assists in water conservation (Siebert et al. 1974) best explained its preference for mesophytic

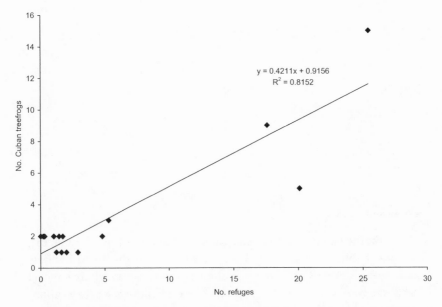

Figure 8.1. Relationship between abundance of Cuban treefrogs and number of refuges on buildings in Everglades National Park during December 1991–November 1992 and July 1995–June 1996. F = 61.2, p < 0.000.

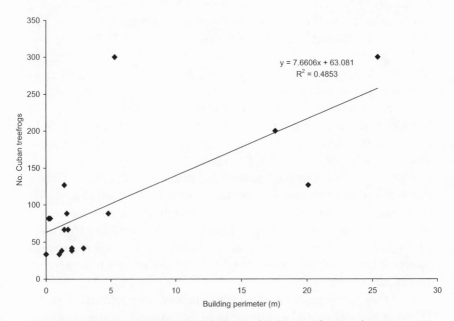

Figure 8.2. Relationship between abundance of Cuban treefrogs and perimeter (m) on buildings in Everglades National Park during December 1991–November 1992 and July 1995–June 1996. F = 14.1, p < 0.002.

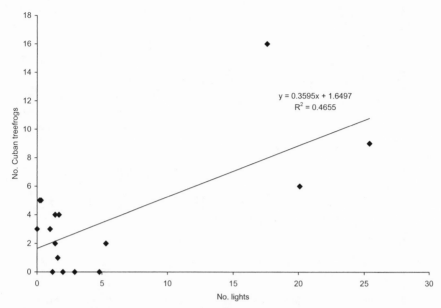

Figure 8.3. Relationship between abundance of Cuban treefrogs and number of lights on buildings in Everglades National Park during December 1991–November 1992 and July 1995–June 1996. F = 13.1, p < 0.003.

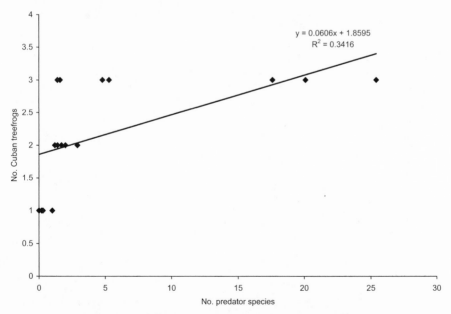

Figure 8.4. Relationship between abundance of Cuban treefrogs and number of predator species on buildings in Everglades National Park during December 1991–November 1992 and July 1995–June 1996. F = 7.8, p < 0.01.

Table 8.1. Relative abundance of the Cuban treefrog, green treefrog, squirrel treefrog, Indo-Pacific gecko, and wood slave in Everglades National Park.

Site	Cuban treefrog	Green treefrog	Squirrel treefrog	Indo-Pacific gecko	Wood slave
TRAILS					
SLOUGH[1]	4.8 ± 3.8	1.2 ± 1.3	1.0 ± 1.0	0.0	0.0
SLOUGH[2]	1.1 ± 0.9	0.4 ± 0.6	0.0	0.0	0.0
MARSH[1]	0.0	5.2 ± 0.2	16.1 ± 21.2	0.0	0.0
RP HAMMOCK[1]	4.1 ± 3.7	0.3 ± 0.4	0.1 ± 0.3	0.0	0.0
RP HAMMOCK[2]	2.7 ± 4.3	0.0	0.1 ± 0.3	0.0	0.0
Ma HAMMOCK[2]	3.0 ± 2.1	0.0	0.0	0.1 ± 0.3	0.0
Mo HAMMOCK[1]	2.9 ± 3.4	0.0	0.0	0.0	0.0
TRANSITIONAL[1]	0.5 ± 0.9	0.4 ± 1.2	0.1 ± 0.3	0.0	0.0
PINELAND[1]	1.4 ± 1.3	0.0	0.0	0.0	0.0
MANGROVE[1]	2.9 ± 2.2	0.2 ± 0.6	0.0	0.2 ± 0.4	0.0
MANGROVE[3]	2.0 ± 1.4	0.0	0.0	0.1 ± 0.3	0.0
SCHINUS[1]	3.0 ± 0.5	0.0	0.0	0.0	0.0
OVERLOOKS					
POND[1]	0.8 ± 1.0	0.4 ± 0.8	0.0	0.2 ± 0.6	0.0
POND[2]	0.4 ± 0.6	1.0 ± 1.5	0.0	0.2 ± 0.6	0.0
PRAIRIE[1]	0.3 ± 0.4	1.0 ± 1.6	4.0 ± 3.5	0.0	0.0
MARSH[1]	0.3 ± 0.7	1.4 ± 1.7	3.5 ± 3.1	0.0	0.0
BUILDINGS					
DBC[1]	25.4 ± 18.1	1.7 ± 0.4	0.1 ± 0.3	0.2 ± 0.4	0.0
DBC[2]	5.3 ± 4.0	0.4 ± 1.0	3.9 ± 5.2	0.3 ± 0.4	0.1 ± 0.3
IORI[1]	20.1 ± 28.3	0.1 ± 0.3	0.3 ± 0.4	0.8 ± 1.1	0.0

IORI²	1.4 ± 1.9	0.3 ± 0.4	2.3 ± 4.6	0.2 ± 0.4	0.0
GARAGE¹	4.8 ± 4.0	0.0	0.0	0.3 ± 0.6	0.0
GARAGE²	1.6 ± 2.0	0.0	0.4 ± 0.8	0.0	0.0
LPK	17.6 ± 12.3	0.3 ± 8.2	0.2 ± 0.4	0.3 ± 0.5	0.5 ± 0.5
WEST LAKE¹	2.9 ± 3.9	0.2 ± 0.4	0.0	0.0	0.0
WEST LAKE³	2.0 ± 1.2	0.0	0.0	0.2 ± 0.4	0.0
POST OFFICE¹	2.0 ± 2.5	0.1 ± 0.3	0.0	1.9 ± 2.1	0.0
POST OFFICE²	1.2 ± 0.7	0.1 ± 0.3	0.0	1.8 ± 0.9	0.5 ± 1.0
FISH HUT¹	1.4 ± 0.9	0.5 ± 0.7	0.0	8.6 ± 2.3	1.2 ± 0.8
FISH HUT²	1.7 ± 0.9	2.5 ± 3.8	0.3 ± 0.8	3.9 ± 3.6	19.4 ± 6.7
GAS STATION¹	1.0 ± 1.6	1.6 ± 2.8	0.0	0.3 ± 0.6	0.0
GAS STATION²	0.0	1.3 ± 1.7	0.1 ± 0.3	0.0	4.1 ± 2.7
MARINA¹	0.3 ± 0.5	0.4 ± 0.9	0.0	1.6 ± 1.4	0.0
MARINA²	0.2 ± 0.4	0.7 ± 1.4	0.2 ± 0.6	1.1 ± 1.3	12.7 ± 6.9

1 = December 1991–November 1992. 2 = July 1995–June 1996. 3 = October 1995–June 1996.

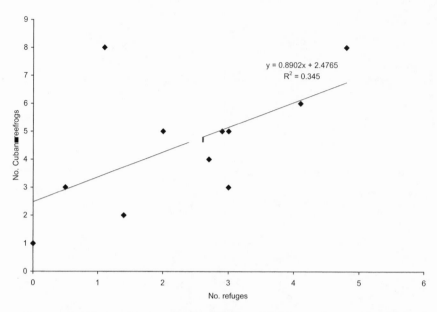

Figure 8.5. Relationship between abundance of Cuban treefrogs and number of refuges on trails in Everglades National Park during December 1991–November 1992 and July 1995–June 1996. F = 5.3, p < 0.05.

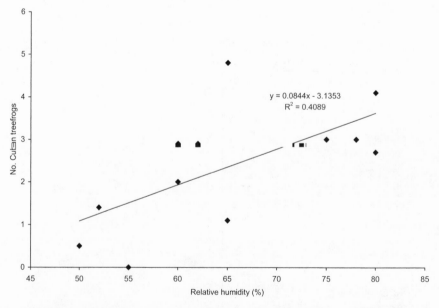

Figure 8.6. Relationship between abundance of Cuban treefrogs and dry season relative humidity (%RH) on trails in Everglades National Park during December 1991–November 1992 and July 1995–June 1996. F = 6.9, p < 0.03.

forest, which maintained higher levels of humidity in the dry season than did other habitats in the park. For those reasons, pinelands, especially those burned frequently, were difficult to invade by the Cuban treefrog. Wetlands were also avoided except along the edges of hammocks and pineland, where suitable breeding sites and hylid prey were present. With the exception of edge habitat, wetlands were seasonally too wet or too dry, lacked vertical structure for hunting, lacked acceptable refuges, and were unsuitable for reproduction.

Among overlooks, the limited use of prairie as larval sites was seasonal on the very edges of uplands. The Cuban treefrog was significantly less numerous ($t_{df = 12} = 1.8$, $P < 0.009$) during 1991–1992 than during 1995–1996, an interval that was overlapped by two high-water years. Its aversion to high water was also evident in its absence in sawgrass marsh. Because of overwhelming numbers of predators of tadpoles and postmetamorphic individuals as well as a dearth of refuges, this habitat—essentially an ocean between hammock islands—precludes colonization by the Cuban treefrog.

Its affinity for buildings, disturbed habitat, and forests that I observed in the park was also apparent everywhere else I looked. In Palmdale, Florida, for instance, I collected postmetamorphic individuals from buildings and vegetation at a campground along Fisheating Creek. In Okeechobee and Lake Placid, I collected almost all of them from a few reliable buildings. My Tampa collection came dependably from a botanical garden at the University of South Florida and from two residences in Temple Terrace. Although individuals were heard calling from hammocks in Key Largo, the Torch keys, and Big Pine Key, daytime collections from nurseries and nighttime collections from buildings accounted for Florida Keys specimens.

In Cuba, I collected a series of 67 individuals in a few days in June almost exclusively from buildings and adjacent vegetation in and around Havana. In this regard, its association with humanity, banana groves in particular, gave rise to its common name *rana platanera* (banana frog) in Cuba. As in Florida, although highly successful around human habitations, the Cuban treefrog in Cuba also does well in naturally wooded areas, generally avoiding deep forest (Barbour and Ramsden 1919). It is also present in mangrove forest (L. Moreno, pers. comm.).

In George Town, Grand Cayman, Cuban treefrogs were difficult *not* to see on buildings and in cisterns during summer nights. On New Providence Island, I caught them by day in the axils of palms along roadsides, and on buildings by night.

Contrary to the terrestrial habitat affinity of the Cuban treefrog, habitats of the green treefrog (*Hyla cinerea*) and squirrel treefrog (*H. squirella*) in the park were primarily freshwater wetlands (table 8.1) where their abundances along trails were strongly associated with one another (r = 0.98, P < 0.0000; N = 12). Although these two native species were semi-aquatic, some habitat differences existed between them. The green treefrog was most abundant around permanent water, whereas the more abundant squirrel treefrog preferred seasonally flooded systems (table 8.1).

Neither of these native treefrogs fared well with the Cuban treefrog in upland, wetland, or building habitats. For example, colonization of Mahogany Hammock by the Cuban treefrog was associated with an immediate reduction in numbers of both native hylids, despite an already marginal presence (table 8.2). After I observed the first Cuban treefrog, a female (86.3 mm SVL), on 9 June 1992, and heard the first chorus of the Cuban treefrog on my next visit of 24 June 1992, I no longer saw green treefrogs and squirrel treefrogs in the hammock and only occasionally heard them in the hammock, yet I still heard both species in the marsh surrounding the hammock. During 1995–1996, the Cuban treefrog was still present to the exclusion of the two native hylid species (table 8.1). Along Anhinga Trail, the green treefrog and squirrel treefrog co-occurred with the Cuban treefrog but at relative abundances that were much lower than those in marshes and prairies that lacked their predator (table 8.1). The negative relationship between both hylids and the Cuban treefrog was more readily detectable in the squirrel treefrog data than in those of the green treefrog, perhaps because of the squirrel treefrog's greater abundance in the park. For example, the decrease in numbers of the Cuban treefrog at DBC during 1995–1996 was associated with an increase in the abundance of the squirrel treefrog ($t_{df=11}$ =-2.37, P < 0.04).

The Indo-Pacific gecko (*Hemidactylus garnotii*) was nearly an exclusive building-dwelling species in the park (table 8.1). Its presence at Eco Pond was marginal, perhaps associated with the boardwalk. The presence of the Indo-Pacific gecko at West Lake overlapped the duration of repair of a three-meter length of boardwalk. Only one individual was observed along the Gumbo Limbo Trail during this study.

The wood slave (*H. mabouia*) was found on buildings and surrounding vegetation, having rapidly colonized buildings at Flamingo since the 1991–1992 season (table 8.1) to the detriment of the Indo-Pacific gecko (Meshaka 2000).

Table 8.2. Number of individuals of the Cuban treefrog, green treefrog, and squirrel treefrog, observed in Mahogany Hammock from three time periods.

	Time Periods		
Species	1	2	3
Cuban treefrog	0.0 + 0.0	4.5 ± 3.9	3.0 ± 2.1
Green treefrog	0.1 + 0.3	0.0 + 0.0	0.0 + 0.0
Squirrel treefrog	0.1 + 0.3	0.0 + 0.0	0.0 + 0.0

1. June 1991–May 1992.
2. June–November 1992.
3. July 1995–January 1996.
Means are followed by ± one standard deviation.

With very few exceptions, exotic amphibians and reptiles in Florida occur only on buildings and in disturbed habitats (Meshaka et al. 2001). Exceptionally, the brown anole (*Anolis sagrei*) and greenhouse frog (*Eleutherodactylus planirostris planirostris*) readily invade natural habitats in Florida, and both species are geographically widespread in the state (Meshaka et al. 2001). In the West Indies I have heard choruses of the greenhouse frog and the eastern narrowmouth toad (*Gastrophryne carolinensis*) in George Town, Grand Cayman, and the southern leopard frog (*Rana sphenocephala*) in a rural setting on New Providence Island.

9

Diet

Dietary niche breadth

In the park, the Cuban treefrog ate seemingly every manner of terrestrial invertebrate prey and an impressive array of vertebrates, but its dietary niche was generally intermediate in breadth at the species level, for both sexes, and for juveniles (table 9.1). The highest values of niche breadth were recorded from buildings, where this species was adept at exploiting high numbers of light-attracted prey.

Generally speaking, the Cuban treefrog fed numerically most heavily on beetles (Coleoptera), roaches (Blattaria), and roly-polies (Isopoda: Armadillidaridae) (table 9.2). Another way I measured diet was by counting the number of stomachs in which each prey taxon or category occurred. Using this measure of diet, the Cuban treefrog ate mostly beetles, roaches, caterpillars (larval Lepidoptera), and moths (Lepidoptera). Common to both of these measures of diet were beetles and roaches. Beetles, especially the light-attracted forms, were the treefrog's primary prey on buildings, whereas roaches were its dominant prey in nature. More specifically, males ate mostly beetles and moths on buildings and ate spiders (Araneae) and beetles in nature (table 9.3). Females ate primarily beetles and earwigs (Dermaptera: Labiidae) on buildings and roaches and spiders in nature (table 9.4). From a smaller series, beetles were most common in the diet of juveniles from buildings and nature (table 9.5). By either measure of diet, males and juveniles were beetle-eaters, and females were beetle- and roach-eaters. These forms figured prominently across sites; however, some exceptions were found. For example, earwigs, roly-polies, and lepidopterans, especially moths, appeared in high numbers on some buildings.

On buildings in the Florida Keys a few adults had eaten mostly roaches (Meshaka 1996g). West Indian populations also feed predominantly on

Table 9.1. Niche breadths of the Cuban treefrog, green treefrog, squirrel treefrog, Indo-Pacific gecko, and wood slave, from Everglades National Park.

Species	Buildings			Nature	Buildings and nature	N
	HID & LPK	FLAM & WLB	All			
Cuban treefrog						
Males	31(49)	64(64)	30(49)	29(58)	38(51)	111
Females	50(56)	52(64)	48(53)	37(39)	48(48)	291
Juveniles	57(49)	34(91)	53(47)	34(61)	45(46)	25
All	41(47)	54(60)	41(48)	41(43)	41(46)	427
Green treefrog	14(44)	40(40)	20(38)	38(52)	18(35)	67
Squirrel treefrog	38(35)	N.A.	38(35)	11(37)	20(38)	64
Indo-Pacific gecko	54(57)	14(39)	25(51)	74(86)*	23(51)	48
Wood slave	N.A.	14(46)**	16(49)	N.A.	16(49)	35

Niche breadth as measured by number of prey is followed in parentheses by that of numbers of stomachs containing each category and presented as a percentage.
* N = 4.
** FLAM only.
N.A. Not available because N = 1.

Table 9.2. Diet of all Cuban treefrogs from buildings, nature, and combined sites in Everglades National Park.

Prey	Building	Nature	All sites
Areneida	26(20)	40(34)	66(54)
Coleoptera	175(79)	47(39)	222(118)
Dermaptera	70(29)	8(6)	78(35)
Dictyoptera	29(26)	74(65)	103(91)
Diptera	50(16)	11(4)	61(20)
Hemiptera	51(27)	16(10)	67(37)
Homoptera	24(9)	8(7)	32(16)
Hymenoptera	28(20)	14(11)	42(31)
Isoptera	9(2)	8(4)	17(6)
Lepidoptera	73(36)	29(27)	102(63)
Odonata	2(2)	2(2)	4(4)
Orthoptera	51(30)	25(22)	76(52)
Trichoptera	9(3)	0(0)	9(3)
Gastropoda	23(19)	9(9)	32(28)
Isopoda	57(24)	57(16)	114(40)
Chilopoda	1(1)	3(3)	4(4)
Diplopoda	0(0)	1(1)	1(1)
Oligochaeta	0(0)	1(1)	1(1)
Anura	21(20)	20(20)	41(40)
Squamata	2(2)	1(1)	3(3)
Skin	10(10)	4(4)	14(14)
Vegetation	1(1)	1(1)	2(2)
Stones	4(2)	0(0)	4(2)
Sum	716(378)	379(287)	1,095(665)
Count	21	21	23

Number of prey are followed in parentheses by number of stomachs containing categories of prey.

Table 9.3. Diet of male Cuban treefrogs from all sites in Everglades National Park.

Prey	LPKB	HID	FLAM	MANG	PINE	HAMM	SLOU	SCHIN	TOTAL
	10	41	8	5	8	16	4	19	111
Areneida	1(1)	6(4)	0(0)	2(2)	1(1)	5(4)	1(1)	4(3)	20(16)
Coleoptera	6(5)	61(15)	1(1)	0(0)	2(2)	2(2)	2(1)	9(8)	83(34)
Dermaptera	0(0)	7(4)	0(0)	0(0)	0(0)	0(0)	0(0)	3(2)	10(6)
Dictyoptera	0(0)	6(6)	0(0)	0(0)	4(4)	2(2)	0(0)	3(2)	15(14)
Diptera	18(3)	0(0)	0(0)	0(0)	0(0)	0(0)	0(0)	1(1)	19(4)
Hemiptera	3(2)	3(2)	1(1)	1(1)	0(0)	3(1)	0(0)	8(4)	19(11)
Homoptera	5(1)	0(0)	0(0)	0(0)	0(0)	0(0)	0(0)	0(0)	5(1)
Hymenoptera	0(0)	3(1)	0(0)	0(0)	0(0)	1(1)	0(0)	1(1)	5(3)
Isoptera	0(0)	1(1)	0(0)	0(0)	1(1)	5(1)	0(0)	0(0)	7(3)
Lepidoptera	19(4)	8(7)	2(2)	0(0)	1(1)	2(2)	1(1)	1(1)	34(18)
Orthoptera	0(0)	3(3)	4(4)	0(0)	1(1)	4(4)	0(0)	0(0)	12(12)
Trichoptera	5(1)	0(0)	0(0)	0(0)	0(0)	0(0)	0(0)	0(0)	5(1)
Gastropoda	2(2)	7(5)	0(0)	0(0)	0(0)	1(1)	0(0)	0(0)	10(8)
Isopoda	0(0)	11(7)	0(0)	3(2)	0(0)	0(0)	0(0)	48(11)	62(20)
Chilopoda	0(0)	1(1)	0(0)	0(0)	0(0)	1(1)	0(0)	2(2)	4(4)
Anura	0(0)	2(2)	0(0)	0(0)	0(0)	1(1)	1(1)	0(0)	4(4)
Vegetation	0(0)	0(0)	0(0)	0(0)	0(0)	1(1)	0(0)	0(0)	1(1)
Sum	59(19)	119(58)	8(8)	6(5)	10(10)	28(21)	5(4)	80(35)	315(160)
Count	8	13	4	3	6	12	4	10	17

Number of prey are followed in parentheses by number of stomachs containing categories of prey.

Table 9.4. Diet of female Cuban treefrogs from all sites in Everglades National Park.

Prey	LPKB	HID	FLAM	WLB	POND	MANG	PINE	PRAI	HAMM	SLOU	SCHIN	TOTAL
	27	90	14	15	2	33	4	1	43	58	4	291
Araneida	1(1)	15(11)	0(0)	1(1)	0(0)	10(8)	0(0)	0(0)	6(6)	8(6)	1(1)	42(34)
Coleoptera	9(9)	73(30)	5(3)	6(4)	0(0)	4(4)	2(2)	0(0)	8(8)	5(4)	2(2)	114(66)
Dermoptera	3(2)	59(22)	0(0)	1(1)	0(0)	3(2)	0(0)	0(0)	0(0)	1(1)	1(1)	68(29)
Dictyoptera	5(4)	12(10)	0(0)	6(6)	0(0)	9(9)	0(0)	0(0)	29(24)	24(21)	1(1)	86(75)
Diptera	5(4)	8(4)	0(0)	2(2)	0(0)	0(0)	0(0)	0(0)	10(3)	0(0)	0(0)	25(13)
Hemiptera	4(2)	19(5)	7(6)	4(2)	0(0)	1(1)	0(0)	0(0)	1(1)	1(1)	0(0)	37(18)
Homoptera	5(2)	4(4)	0(0)	0(0)	0(0)	2(1)	0(0)	0(0)	2(2)	3(3)	0(0)	16(12)
Hymenoptera	7(3)	15(13)	2(2)	1(1)	0(0)	6(4)	0(0)	0(0)	0(0)	3(3)	2(1)	36(27)
Isoptera	8(1)	0(0)	0(0)	0(0)	0(0)	0(0)	0(0)	0(0)	2(2)	0(0)	0(0)	10(3)
Lepidoptera	3(3)	34(15)	2(2)	0(0)	0(0)	4(4)	1(1)	0(0)	5(4)	11(10)	1(1)	61(40)
Odonata	0(0)	1(1)	0(0)	0(0)	0(0)	0(0)	0(0)	0(0)	1(1)	1(1)	0(0)	3(3)
Orthoptera	5(5)	34(13)	0(0)	3(3)	0(0)	6(4)	0(0)	0(0)	5(4)	6(6)	1(1)	60(36)
Trichoptera	3(1)	1(1)	0(0)	0(0)	0(0)	0(0)	0(0)	0(0)	0(0)	0(0)	0(0)	4(2)
Gastropoda	4(3)	7(6)	2(2)	1(1)	0(0)	1(1)	1(1)	0(0)	3(3)	3(3)	0(0)	22(20)
Isopoda	2(1)	40(14)	3(1)	0(0)	0(0)	3(1)	0(0)	0(0)	0(0)	0(0)	2(1)	50(18)
Diplopoda	0(0)	0(0)	0(0)	0(0)	0(0)	0(0)	0(0)	0(0)	1(1)	0(0)	0(0)	1(1)
Oligochaeta	0(0)	0(0)	0(0)	0(0)	0(0)	0(0)	0(0)	0(0)	0(0)	1(1)	0(0)	1(1)
Anura	2(2)	15(14)	1(1)	1(1)	1(1)	2(2)	0(0)	1(1)	3(3)	11(11)	0(0)	37(36)
Squamata	0(0)	1(1)	1(1)	0(0)	0(0)	0(0)	0(0)	0(0)	0(0)	1(1)	0(0)	3(3)
Skin	3(3)	3(3)	3(3)	1(1)	1(1)	2(2)	0(0)	0(0)	0(0)	1(1)	0(0)	14(14)
Vegetation	0(0)	0(0)	1(1)	0(0)	0(0)	0(0)	0(0)	0(0)	0(0)	0(0)	0(0)	1(1)
Stones	0(0)	4(2)	0(0)	0(0)	0(0)	0(0)	0(0)	0(0)	0(0)	0(0)	0(0)	4(2)
Sum	69(46)	345(169)	27(22)	27(23)	2(2)	53(43)	4(4)	1(1)	76(62)	80(73)	11(9)	695(454)
Count	16	18	10	11	2	13	3	1	13	15	8	22

Number of prey are followed in parentheses by number of stomachs containing categories of prey.

Table 9.5. Diet of juvenile Cuban treefrogs from all sites in Everglades National Park.

Prey	LPKB	HID	FLAM	WLB	MANG	PINE	HAMM	SLOU	SCHI	TOTAL
	5	2	2	1	5	1	4	3	2	25
Areneida	0(0)	1(1)	1(1)	0(0)	0(0)	0(0)	2(2)	0(0)	0(0)	4(4)
Coleoptera	12(10)	0(0)	1(1)	1(1)	4(4)	1(1)	0(0)	6(1)	0(0)	25(18)
Dictyoptera	0(0)	0(0)	0(0)	0(0)	0(0)	0(0)	1(1)	0(0)	1(1)	2(2)
Diptera	9(2)	0(0)	8(1)	0(0)	0(0)	0(0)	0(0)	0(0)	0(0)	17(3)
Hemiptera	9(6)	0(0)	1(1)	0(0)	0(0)	0(0)	0(0)	0(0)	1(1)	11(8)
Homoptera	10(2)	0(0)	0(0)	0(0)	0(0)	0(0)	1(1)	0(0)	0(0)	11(3)
Hymenoptera	0(0)	0(0)	0(0)	0(0)	1(1)	0(0)	0(0)	0(0)	0(0)	1(1)
Lepidoptera	4(2)	0(0)	1(1)	0(0)	1(1)	0(0)	0(0)	1(1)	0(0)	7(5)
Odonata	0(0)	0(0)	1(1)	0(0)	0(0)	0(0)	0(0)	0(0)	0(0)	1(1)
Orthoptera	1(1)	1(1)	0(0)	0(0)	0(0)	0(0)	1(1)	1(1)	0(0)	4(4)
Isopoda	0(0)	1(1)	0(0)	0(0)	1(1)	0(0)	0(0)	0(0)	0(0)	2(2)
Sum	45(23)	3(3)	13(6)	1(1)	7(7)	1(1)	5(5)	8(3)	2(2)	85(51)
Count	6	3	6	1	4	1	4	3	2	11

Number of prey are followed in parentheses by number of stomachs containing categories of prey.

roaches and isopods, and the dietary niche breadths of both sexes are intermediate (< 0.50) or low (Meshaka 1996g).

The dietary niche breadth of the four competitors in the park was generally narrower than that of the Cuban treefrog, regardless of the collection site, sex, or size-class of Cuban treefrog (table 9.1). Diet of its potential competitors also comprised different primary prey (table 9.1). For example, both the green treefrog, *Hyla cinerea* (table 9.6), and squirrel treefrog, *H. squirella* (table 9.7), fed mostly on flies (Diptera), beetles, and true bugs (Hemiptera), with the latter two prey especially abundant in the stomachs of samples from buildings. Flies were far and away the primary prey of both geckos (tables 9.8, 9.9), and hymenopterans (ants) or beetles fell a distant second place in their diets.

Many of the insectivorous species of amphibians and reptiles in Florida also eat a lot of beetles. Exceptionally, a few of the anoles and the marine toad (*Bufo marinus*) eat an enormous number of ants (Meshaka et al. 2001), and one species, the bark anole (*Anolis distichus*), favors ants. However, very few of the insectivorous exotic species of amphibians and reptiles in Florida include roaches in their diet more than passingly. The notable exception is the tokay gecko (*Gekko gecko*), which, like the Cuban treefrog, eats lots of roaches and beetles (Meshaka et al. 1997, 2001). For this reason, I believe that among the exotic herpetofauna of Florida, the tokay gecko comes closest as a true competitor of the Cuban treefrog for food. In the West Indies, *O. dominicensis* eats many of the same prey as the Cuban treefrog, but especially beetles and orthopterans (Duer et al. 1993).

Dietary niche overlap

What might seem like smaller overlap between the Cuban treefrog and its competitors than among its competitors was true. The Cuban treefrog overlapped greatly with itself between buildings and natural sites (table 9.10). Even broken down by sex and size-class, and then compared between sites, this species ate quite a bit of the same prey. Because the prey on buildings was biased toward similar small-bodied, light-attracted prey edible by most size-classes, overlap in the diet between the sexes was higher on buildings than in nature. Juveniles, closer in body size to males, shared the food resource more with males than with females. Buildings were trophically different enough from nature that diet compared between sexes on a building was more similar than was the diet compared between males in nature and on buildings.

Table 9.6. Diet of all green treefrogs from all sites in Everglades National Park.

Prey	HID	GLTB	FLAM	WLB	MANG	POND	HAM	PRAI	MAR	SLOU	Total
	6	3	13	6	8	1	9	1	11	9	67
Araneida	2(1)	0(0)	0(0)	7(1)	3(2)	0(0)	1(1)	0(0)	5(5)	0(0)	18(10)
Coleoptera	32(11)	2(2)	11(8)	16(6)	3(3)	1(1)	0(0)	1(1)	3(3)	17(7)	86(42)
Dictyoptera	0(0)	0(0)	0(0)	0(0)	1(1)	0(0)	1(1)	0(0)	0(0)	0(0)	2(2)
Diptera	133(5)	0(0)	4(1)	25(3)	0(0)	0(0)	2(2)	0(0)	3(1)	28(5)	195(17)
Hemiptera	10(4)	0(0)	25(6)	4(2)	1(1)	0(0)	0(0)	0(0)	1(1)	0(0)	41(14)
Homoptera	4(3)	0(0)	1(1)	0(0)	9(1)	0(0)	0(0)	0(0)	0(0)	1(1)	15(6)
Hymenoptera	10(3)	0(0)	2(2)	3(2)	1(1)	0(0)	2(2)	0(0)	0(0)	3(3)	21(13)
Isoptera	0(0)	0(0)	0(0)	1(1)	0(0)	0(0)	0(0)	0(0)	0(0)	0(0)	1(1)
Lepidoptera	7(2)	0(0)	1(1)	1(1)	1(1)	0(0)	1(1)	0(0)	2(1)	0(0)	13(7)
Odonata	1(1)	0(0)	0(0)	0(0)	0(0)	0(0)	0(0)	0(0)	0(0)	0(0)	1(1)
Orthoptera	1(1)	1(1)	1(1)	0(0)	0(0)	0(0)	3(2)	0(0)	0(0)	0(0)	6(5)
Thysanura	0(0)	0(0)	0(0)	0(0)	0(0)	0(0)	1(1)	0(0)	0(0)	0(0)	1(1)
Gastropoda	0(0)	0(0)	0(0)	0(0)	1(1)	0(0)	0(0)	0(0)	0(0)	0(0)	1(1)
Isopoda	8(1)	0(0)	0(0)	0(0)	7(2)	0(0)	0(0)	0(0)	0(0)	0(0)	15(3)
Vegetation	0(0)	0(0)	0(0)	0(0)	0(0)	0(0)	1(1)	0(0)	3(3)	0(0)	4(4)
Skin	0(0)	0(0)	0(0)	0(0)	1(1)	0(0)	1(1)	0(0)	1(1)	0(0)	3(3)
Sum	208(32)	3(3)	45(20)	57(16)	28(14)	1(1)	13(12)	1(1)	18(15)	49(16)	423(130)
Count	10	2	7	7	10	1	9	1	7	4	16

Number of prey are followed in parentheses by number of stomachs containing categories of prey.

Table 9.7. Diet of all squirrel treefrogs from all sites in Everglades National Park.

	HID	LPKB	MAR	SLOU	PRAI	TOTAL
Prey	27	7	24	4	2	64
Areneida	12(7)	7(3)	38(9)	2(1)	0(0)	59(20)
Coleoptera	67(30)	4(3)	10(7)	2(1)	5(2)	88(43)
Dictyoptera	0(0)	1(1)	0(0)	0(0)	0(0)	1(1)
Diptera	61(16)	20(6)	233(13)	8(3)	0(0)	322(38)
Ephemoptera	13(1)	0(0)	4(2)	0(0)	0(0)	17(3)
Hemiptera	50(29)	5(2)	0(0)	0(0)	0(0)	55(31)
Homoptera	31(12)	4(2)	21(3)	0(0)	0(0)	56(17)
Hymenoptera	28(7)	2(1)	0(0)	10(2)	0(0)	40(10)
Isoptera	3(2)	0(0)	0(0)	0(0)	0(0)	3(2)
Lepidoptera	2(1)	1(1)	0(0)	1(1)	0(0)	4(3)
Orthoptera	1(1)	0(0)	1(1)	0(0)	0(0)	2(2)
Psocoptera	1(1)	0(0)	0(0)	0(0)	0(0)	1(1)
Trichoptera	0(0)	2(1)	1(1)	0(0)	0(0)	3(2)
Isopoda	6(1)	0(0)	0(0)	0(0)	0(0)	6(1)
Sum	275(108)	46(20)	308(36)	23(8)	5(2)	657(174)
Count	12	9	7	5	1	14

Number of prey are followed in parentheses by number of stomachs containing categories of prey.

Table 9.8. Diet of all Indo-Pacific geckos from all sites in Everglades National Park.

	HID	LPKB	FLM	WLB	MANG	POND	TOTAL
Prey	6	2	34	2	2	2	48
Areneida	1(1)	0(0)	6(5)	1(1)	1(1)	2(1)	11(9)
Coleoptera	3(2)	4(4)	8(3)	2(2)	0(0)	2(1)	19(12)
Dermaptera	2(1)	0(0)	0(0)	0(0)	0(0)	0(0)	2(1)
Dictyoptera	1(1)	1(1)	2(2)	0(0)	0(0)	0(0)	4(4)
Diptera	2(1)	0(0)	78(21)	0(0)	0(0)	1(1)	81(23)
Hemiptera	0(0)	0(0)	3(3)	0(0)	0(0)	0(0)	3(3)
Homoptera	6(4)	4(2)	3(2)	0(0)	0(0)	0(0)	13(8)
Hymenoptera	1(1)	0(0)	15(10)	0(0)	0(0)	0(0)	16(11)
Isoptera	0(0)	0(0)	3(2)	0(0)	0(0)	0(0)	3(2)
Lepidoptera	2(2)	3(2)	3(3)	0(0)	0(0)	0(0)	8(7)
Orthoptera	0(0)	0(0)	3(3)	0(0)	1(1)	0(0)	4(4)
Isopoda	0(0)	0(0)	2(1)	0(0)	0(0)	0(0)	2(1)
Stones	0(0)	0(0)	1(1)	0(0)	0(0)	0(0)	1(1)
Sum	18(13)	12(9)	127(56)	3(3)	2(2)	5(3)	167(86)
Count	8	4	12	2	2	3	13

Number of prey are followed in parentheses by number of stomachs containing categories of prey.

Table 9.9. Diet of all wood slaves from all sites in Everglades National Park.

	FLAM	LPKB	TOTAL
Prey	34	1	35
Areneida	7(7)	1(1)	8(8)
Coleoptera	9(9)	0(0)	9(9)
Dictyoptera	2(2)	0(0)	2(2)
Diptera	80(20)	0(0)	80(20)
Hemiptera	3(2)	0(0)	3(2)
Homoptera	5(5)	5(3)	10(8)
Hymenoptera	13(8)	0(0)	13(8)
Thysanura	1(1)	0(0)	1(1)
Trichoptera	2(2)	0(0)	2(2)
Gastropoda	3(3)	0(0)	3(3)
Stones	2(1)	0(0)	2(1)
Sum	127(60)	6(4)	133(64)
Count	11	2	11

Number of prey are followed in parentheses by number of stomachs containing categories of prey.

Table 9.10. Dietary overlap expressed as a percent within the Cuban treefrog in Everglades National Park.

	Building	Nature
Building		
Male vs. female	66(78)	
Male vs. juvenile	56(60)	
Female vs. juvenile	48(52)	
Female vs. female		60(65)
Male vs. male		45(70)
Juvenile vs. juvenile		47(69)
Total vs. total		66(75)
Nature		
Male vs. female		46(60)
Male vs. juvenile		46(69)
Female vs. juvenile		54(60)

Dietary overlap as measured by number of prey is followed in parentheses by number of stomachs containing each prey category.

Table 9.11. Percent overlap of the diet of the Cuban treefrog, green treefrog, squirrel treefrog, Indo-Pacific gecko, and wood slave, from all sites combined in Everglades National Park.

Cuban treefrog				
Species	Male	Female	Juvenile	All
Green treefrog	45(54)	47(53)	68(78)	55(56)
Squirrel treefrog	38(49)	39(43)	58(73)	41(48)
Indo-Pacific gecko	42(54)	43(57)	57(57)	44(57)
Wood slave	31(41)	31(45)	45(38)	33(43)

Percent overlap as measured by number of prey is followed in parentheses by that of numbers of stomachs containing each category and presented as a percentage.

From small samples, dietary overlap between the sexes on buildings in Cuba was even higher, at least 80 percent, by either measure of diet (Meshaka 1996g). In George Town, Grand Cayman, dietary overlap between the sexes was at least 50 percent (Meshaka 1996g). At the species level, the Cuban treefrog overlapped with its potential competitors somewhat less than it did intraspecifically (table 9.11). For combined sites at the species level, interspecific overlap was highest with the green treefrog and lowest with the wood slave (table 9.11). With respect to males, females, and juveniles of the Cuban treefrog, interspecific overlap was greatest with juveniles (table 9.11).

However, with the exception of juvenile Cuban treefrog–native treefrog overlaps being high (table 9.11), none of the other comparisons—Cuban treefrog–Cuban treefrog or Cuban treefrog–competitor—approached the level of overlap that existed among the competitors, especially between congenerics. The weakest of these comparisons, green treefrog–wood slave (*Hemidactylus mabouia*), I believe can be explained by the fact that, although flies were most common in the stomachs of the green treefrog, flies did not dominate to the extent that they did in the diets of the other three species. Likewise, when I separated by site the comparisons of dietary overlap, I found greater overlap among the competitors with one another than with the Cuban treefrog (table 9.12). In short, dietary overlap was greater among sex and size-class categories of Cuban treefrogs and among its competitors than it was between the Cuban treefrog and its competitors, such that at the species level the Cuban treefrog and its competitors occupied two different trophic positions.

Table 9.12. Percent overlap of the diet of the Cuban treefrog (CTF), green treefrog (GTF), squirrel treefrog (STF), Indo-Pacific gecko (IPG), and wood slave (WS), from buildings and natural sites in Everglades National Park.

Comparison	Building	Nature
CTF vs. GTF	37(48)[1a]	43(53)[3a]
CTF vs. STF	51(50)[1b]	25(30)[3b]
CTF vs. IPG	59(58)[1b]	
CTF vs. IPG	20(25)[2a]	
CTF vs. IPG	38(41)[2b]	
CTF vs. WS	17(28)[2a]	
GTF vs. STF	53(78)[1a]	62(66)[3c]
GTF vs. IPG	37(49)[1a]	24(38)[4]
GTF vs. IPG	53(51)[2b]	
GTF vs. WS	26(34)[2a]	
STF vs. IPG	46(55)[1b]	
IPG vs. WS	89(76)[2a]	

Overlap as measured by number of prey is followed in parentheses by that of numbers of stomachs containing each category and presented as a percentage.
[1a] Buildings of HID only.
[1b] Buildings of Long Pine Key and Hole in the Donut.
[2a] Buildings of Flamingo only.
[2b] Buildings of West Lake and Flamingo.
[3a] Exclusive of marshes.
[3b] Slough and prairie only.
[3c] Marsh, slough, and prairie only.
[4] Pond and mangrove only.

As mentioned in the preceding section, in Florida the tokay gecko shares with the Cuban treefrog the greatest overlap in diet. Perhaps, then, at least in disturbed habitat, the tokay gecko could obstruct colonization by the Cuban treefrog.

Prey size

The overwhelming preference for roaches and beetles by the Cuban treefrog as compared with its competitors' preference for flies was reflected in a similar separation in prey size and number of prey between the Cuban treefrog and its competitors. Body size (table 9.13), mean prey size (table 9.14), and number of prey (table 9.15) differed among sexes and size-classes of the Cuban treefrog and among the five species (table 9.16). Simply because of their larger body size, it was not surprising that among Cuban treefrogs, whether on buildings or in nature, females ate larger prey than either males or juveniles. As measured by maximum prey size,

Table 9.13. Body size in snout-vent length (mm SVL) of the Cuban treefrog, green treefrog, squirrel treefrog, Indo-Pacific gecko, and wood slave from Everglades National Park.

Species	Building	Nature	Total
Cuban treefrog			
Male	45.1 ± 6.1; 28.6–54.0; 55	44.5 ± 3.9; 37.5–53.5; 37	44.8 ± 5.3; 28.6–54.0; 92
Female	65.4 ± 10.6;44.5–92.0; 117	68.7 ± 12.3; 44.0–93.8;112	67.0 ± 11.5; 44.0–93.8; 229
Juvenile	38.9 ± 5.4; 24.0–43.5; 10	38.5 ± 3.8; 30.0–43.0; 9	38.7 ± 4.7; 24.0–43.5; 19
All	57.8 ± 13.8; 24.0–92.0; 182	61.3 ± 15.7; 30.0–93.8; 158	59.4 ± 14.8; 24.0–93.8;340
Green treefrog	40.6 ± 5.8; 28.8–50.0; 15	38.2 ± 7.6; 25.4–53.0; 33	39.0 ± 7.2; 25.4–53.0; 48
Squirrel treefrog	27.5 ± 3.2; 22.0–34.1; 35	23.6 ± 2.3; 16.4–26.9;26	25.9 ± 3.5; 16.4–34.1; 61
Indo-Pacific gecko	47.7 ± 9.6; 28.0–62.0; 35	53.4 ± 3.2; 49.2–57.0; 3	48.4 ± 9.3; 28.0–62.0; 38
Wood slave	49.9 ± 12.4; 21.0–67.0; 28	N. A.	49.9 ± 12.4; 21.0–67.0; 28

Means are followed by standard deviations, range, and sample size.
N.A. Not available.

Table 9.14. Mean prey length (mm) of the Cuban treefrog, green treefrog, squirrel treefrog, Indo-Pacific gecko, and wood slave, from Everglades National Park.

Species	Building	Nature	Total
Cuban treefrog			
Male	9.7 ± 6.0; 1–34; 152	7.4 ± 4.6; 3–31; 107	8.8 ± 5.6; 1–34; 259
Female	12.2 ± 7.8; 2–50; 452	18.0 ± 10.7; 1–69; 172	13.7 ± 9.1; 1–69; 624
Juvenile	5.0 ± 3.2; 1–17; 57	9.0 ± 4.1; 4–19; 23	6.2 ± 3.9; 1–19; 80
All	10.9 ± 7.5; 1–50; 661	13.6 ± 10.0; 1–69; 302	11.7 ± 8.4; 1–69; 963
Green treefrog	4.0 ± 1.7; 1–12; 288	5.5 ± 4.2; 2–20; 105	4.4 ± 2.7; 1–20; 393
Squirrel treefrog	3.9 ± 1.5; 1–10; 304	2.2 ± 1.6; 0.5–12; 334	3.0 ± 1.8; 0.5–12; 638
Indo-Pacific gecko	4.0 ± 2.2; 1–16; 150	5.6 ± 3.1; 2–11; 5	4.1 ± 2.3; 1–16; 155
Wood slave	4.3 ± 2.6; 1–15; 115	N.A.	4.3 ± 2.6; 1–15; 115

Means are followed by standard deviations, range, and sample size.
N.A. Not available.

Table 9.15. Number of prey recovered from the Cuban treefrog, green treefrog, squirrel treefrog, Indo-Pacific gecko, and wood slave, in Everglades National Park.

Species	Building	Nature	Total
Cuban treefrog			
Male	2.8 ± 2.5; 1–11; 55	2.8 ± 2.6; 1–11; 37	2.8 ± 2.6; 1–11; 92
Female	3.9 ± 4.8; 1–24; 117	1.7 ± 1.4; 1–11; 112	2.8 ± 3.8; 1–24; 229
Juvenile	5.7 ± 6.7; 1–19; 10	1.7 ± 0.9; 1–4; 9	3.8 ± 5.3; 1–19; 19
All	3.7 ± 4.5; 1–24; 182	1.9 ± 1.8; 1–11; 158	2.9 ± 3.6; 1–24; 340
Green treefrog	17.3 ± 21.6; 1–86; 15	3.2 ± 3.9; 1–16; 33	7.6 ± 14.6; 1–86; 48
Squirrel treefrog	8.5 ± 5.9; 1–26; 35	12.9 ± 17.7; 1–76; 26	10.4 ± 12.6; 1–76; 61
Indo-Paciifc gecko	4.3 ± 5.2; 1–25; 35	2.0 ± 1.4; 1–4; 3	4.2 ± 5.1; 1–25; 38
Wood slave	4.1 ± 4.9; 1–24; 28	N.A.	4.1 ± 4.9; 1–24; 28

Means are followed by standard deviations, range, and sample size.
N.A. Not available.

Table 9.16. Statistical differences in mean prey length (mm) and number of prey within the Cuban treefrog and between the Cuban treefrog and its competitors in Everglades National Park.

Species	Nature	Building
Body size		
Cuban treefrog		
Cuban treefrog vs. green treefrog	$T_{df=98} = 12.59, P < 0.0000$	$T_{df=28} = 9.17, P < 0.0000$
Cuban treefrog vs. squirrel treefrog	$T_{df=179} = 28.06, P < 0.0000$	$T_{df=209} = 26.10, P < 0.0000$
Cuban treefrog vs. Indo-Pacific gecko	X	$T_{df=64} = 5.21, P < 0.0000$
Cuban treefrog vs. wood slave	X	$T_{df=208} = 2.86, P < 0.002$
Prey length		
Cuban treefrog		
male vs. female	$T_{df=253} = -11.30, P < 0.000$	$T_{df=329} = 3.98, P < 0.0000$
male vs. juvenile	$T = P > 0.05$	$T_{df=184} = 7.12, P < 0.0000$
female vs. juvenile	$T_{df=70} = 7.45, P < 0.0000$	$T_{df=158} = 12.62, P < 0.0000$
Cuban treefrog vs. green treefrog	$T_{df=390} = 11.40, P < 0.0000$	$T_{df=794} = 22.90, P < 0.0000$
Cuban treefrog vs. squirrel treefrog	$T_{df=314} = 19.60, P < 0.0000$	$T_{df=768} = 23.40, P < 0.0000$
Cuban treefrog vs. Indo-Pacific gecko	X	$T_{df=762} = 20.40, P < 0.0000$
Cuban treefrog vs. wood slave	X	$T_{df=504} = 17.70, P < 0.0000$
No. prey		
Cuban treefrog		
male vs. female	$T_{df=43} = 2.33\ P < 0.007$	$T = T_{df=168}\ 2.08\ P < 0.000$
male vs. juvenile	N.S.	N.S.
female vs. juvenile	$T_{df=117} = -18.90\ P < 0.000$	N.S.
Cuban treefrog vs. green treefrog	$T_{df=35} = -1.78, P < 0.04$	$T_{df=24} = -3.40\ P < 0.0000$
Cuban treefrog vs. squirrel treefrog	$T_{df=25} = -1.78, P < 0.0000$	$T_{df=35} = -2.35, P < 0.01$
Cuban treefrog vs. Indo-Pacific gecko	X	N.S.
Cuban treefrog vs. wood slave	X	N.S.

P values of T-test are one-tailed.
X Sample size too small for statistical comparison.
N.S. Not significant.

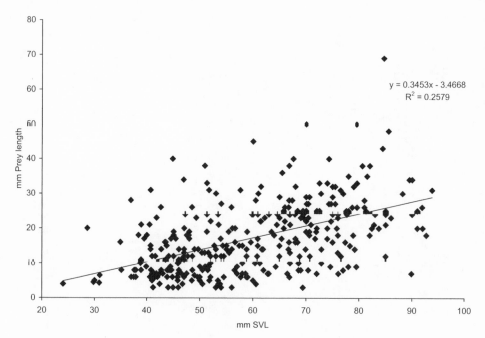

Figure 9.1. Relationship between body size (mm SVL) and maximum prey length (mm) in the Cuban treefrog from Everglades National Park. $F = 117.43$, $p < 0.000$.

for the park Cuban treefrogs, large body size also meant increasingly large-bodied prey (fig. 9.1), as expected in light of the wide range of lengths among prey categories (moth versus roach) and within a prey category (small roach versus big roach). The reward, then, for large body size was the ability to exploit large prey taxa and large individuals of those prey. The most striking examples involved the ability of females to eat more and larger roaches than smaller-bodied males and juveniles. Likewise, in roach-eating populations of the Cuban treefrog in the West Indies, mean or maximum prey length increased with an increase in the body size of the predator (Meshaka 1996g).

In the park, competitors of the Cuban treefrog, because of their reliance on small flies, beetles, and termites, ate smaller prey than the Cuban treefrog both on buildings and in nature. Interspecific differences in gape in relation to maximum prey length illustrate this point (fig. 9.2). Three of the Cuban treefrog's potential competitors (both hylids and the Indo-Pacific gecko) did not increase their maximum prey size with an increase in their own body size (figs. 9.3–9.5), perhaps because of an overall reliance on small-bodied flies in their diet. Exceptionally, the adult wood slaves included large-bodied prey not eaten by smaller conspecifics (fig. 9.6). I

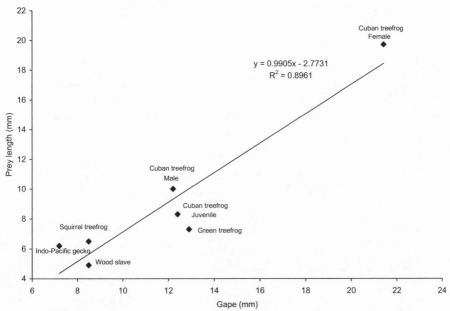

Figure 9.2. Relationship between gape (mm SVL) and maximum prey length (mm) in the Cuban treefrog (males, females, and juveniles), green treefrog, squirrel treefrog, Indo-Pacific gecko, and wood slave from Everglades National Park. $F = 43.14$, $P < 0.001$.

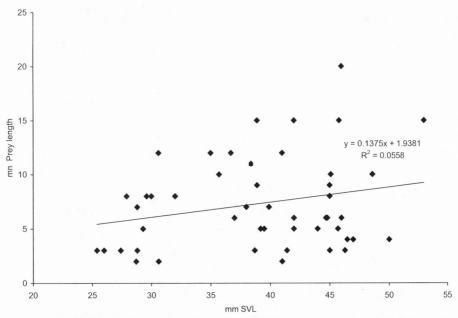

Figure 9.3. Relationship between body size (mm SVL) and maximum prey length (mm) in the green treefrog from Everglades National Park. $F = 1.037$, $P > 0.05$.

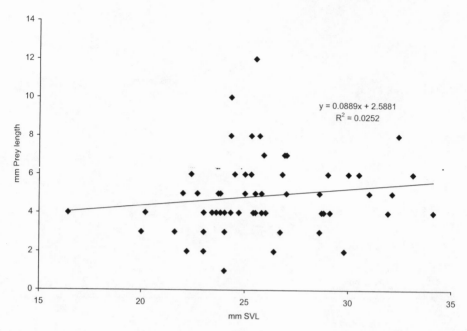

Figure 9.4. Relationship between body size (mm SVL) and maximum prey length (mm) in the squirrel treefrog from Everglades National Park. $F = 1.525$, $p > 0.05$.

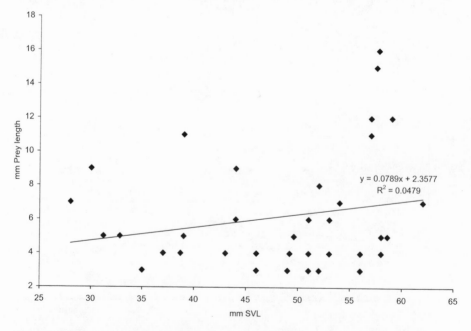

Figure 9.5. Relationship between body size (mm SVL) and maximum prey length (mm) in the Indo-Pacific gecko from Everglades National Park. $F = 1.810$, $p > 0.05$.

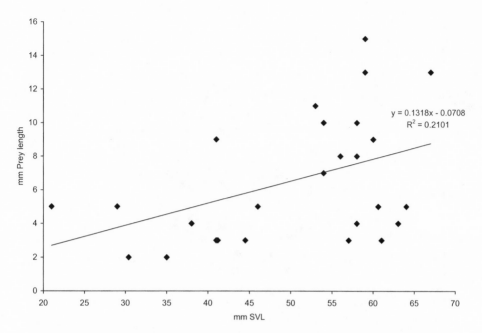

Figure 9.6. Relationship between body size (mm SVL) and maximum prey length (mm) in the wood slave from Everglades National Park. F = 6.916, p < 0.02.

am not sure why that was the case for the wood slave but not the trophically very similar Indo-Pacific gecko (*Hemidactylus garnotii*).

Although these calculations reveal the role of absolute body size as an explanation for prey size differences within the Cuban treefrog and between the five species, they do not determine if such differences existed between similar-sized individuals. In other words, I still did not know if female Cuban treefrogs ate larger prey, per gram of female body weight, than did similar-sized males or juveniles. If the answer were yes, then female Cuban treefrogs were outcompeting males and juveniles for maximum prey size regardless of their body size. If the answer were no, large body size alone accounted for large prey size. Likewise, if I looked at individuals of the five species that were all the same size, were four of them still eating smaller prey than the Cuban treefrog? If they were, then the Cuban treefrog, irrespective of body size, was a superior competitor with respect to the maximum size of prey it could eat. To answer these questions I calculated an ANCOVA, which removed the effect of body size. To maintain homogeneity of variance, I log (ln)-transformed the maximum prey length. For the Cuban treefrog on buildings, the ANCOVA disclosed

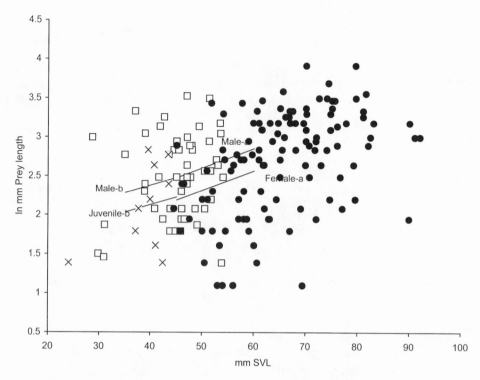

Figure 9.7. Relationship between body size (mm SVL) and maximum prey length (mm) in male (square), female (circle), and juvenile (X) Cuban treefrogs from buildings in Everglades National Park. Adjusted means provide regression lines.

that even with the removal of treefrog body size, that is if males and females were similar in body size, males were eating larger prey than were females (fig. 9.7; tables 9.17, 9.18). No overlap in body size existed between females (45–99 mm SVL) and juveniles (10–45 mm SVL), so I could not determine if the same were true between these two groups as between males and females. However, because range of male body size (27–65 mm SVL) overlapped that of juveniles, I was able to test for body size effects between those two similar-sized groups and found that males and juveniles were trophically similar with respect to maximum prey size even when the effect of body size was removed (fig. 9.7; tables 9.19, 9.20).

In nature, females ate larger prey than did similarly sized males (fig. 9.8; tables 9.21, 9.22). By this same measure males were trophically similar to juveniles (fig. 9.8; tables 9.23, 9.24), which meant that despite a great deal of intraspecific overlap in maximum prey size, there still existed intersexual separation in the prey size that had nothing to do with the size of

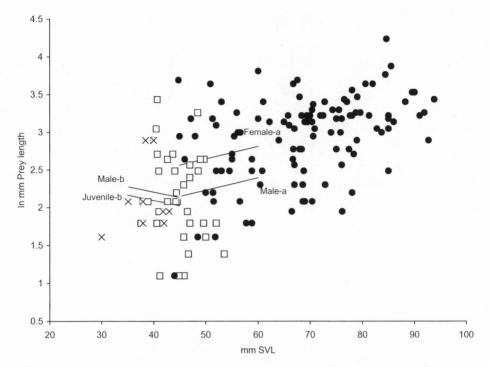

Figure 9.8. Relationship between body size (mm SVL) and maximum prey length (mm) in male (square), female (circle), and juvenile (X) Cuban treefrogs from natural sites in Everglades National Park. Adjusted means provide regression lines.

Table 9.17. Tests of between-subjects effects in the comparison of maximum prey length and number of prey between male and female Cuban treefrogs from buildings in Everglades National Park.

Source	Dependent Variable	Type III Sum of Squares	df	Mean Square	F	Sig.
Corrected Model	Prey length	11.248[a]	2	5.624	17.345	.000
	No. prey	1.231[b]	2	.615	.793	.454
Intercept	Prey length	6.982	1	6.982	21.533	.000
	No. prey	2.630	1	2.630	3.388	.067
SVL	Prey length	9.422	1	9.422	29.059	.000
	No. prey	9.731E-03	1	9.731E-03	.013	.911
Sex	Prey length	1.521	1	1.521	4.690	.032
	No. prey	.499	1	.499	.643	.424
Error	Prey length	54.796	169	.324		
	No. prey	131.198	169	.776		
Total	Prey length	1253.869	172			
	No. prey	247.573	172			
Corrected Total	Prey length	66.044	171			
	No. prey	132.429	171			

Dependent variables are ln-transformed.
[a] R Squared = .170 (Adjusted R Squared = .160)
[b] R Squared = .009 (Adjusted R Squared = -.002)

Table 9.18. Parameter estimates in the comparison of maximum prey length and number of prey between male and female Cuban treefrogs from buildings in Everglades National Park.

Dependent Variable	Parameter	B	Std. Error	t	Sig.	95% Confidence Interval	
						Lower Bound	Upper Bound
Prey length	Intercept	1.064	.308	3.459	.001	.457	1.672
	SVL	2.500E-02	.005	5.391	.000	1.584E-02	3.415E-02
	[Sex=Male]	.287	.132	2.166	.032	2.536E-02	.548
	[Sex=Female]	0a	.	.	.	.	.
No. prey	Intercept	.823	.476	1.730	.086	-.116	1.763
	SVL	8.034E-04	.007	.112	.911	-1.336E-02	1.497E-02
	[Sex=Male]	-.164	.205	-.802	.424	-.569	.240
	[Sex=Female]	0a	.	.	.	.	.

a This parameter is set to zero because it is redundant.

Table 9.19. Tests of between-subjects effects in the comparison of maximum prey length and number of prey between male and juvenile Cuban treefrogs from buildings in Everglades National Park.

Source	Dependent Variable	Type III Sum of Squares	df	Mean Square	F	Sig.
Corrected Model	Prey length	2.019a	2	1.009	3.658	.031
	No. prey	1.475b	2	.738	1.027	.364
Intercept	Prey length	2.771	1	2.771	10.043	.002
	No. prey	.269	1	.269	.374	.543
SVL	Prey length	.871	1	.871	3.157	.081
	No. prey	.238	1	.238	.332	.567
Sex	Prey length	.460	1	.460	1.668	.201
	No. prey	1.471	1	1.471	2.048	.157
Error	Prey length	17.108	62	.276		
	No. prey	44.527	62	.718		
Total	Prey length	400.100	65			
	No. prey	82.968	65			
Corrected Total	Prey length	19.126	64			
	No. prey	46.003	64			

Dependent variables are ln-transformed.
[a] R Squared = .106 (Adjusted R Squared = .077)
[b] R Squared = .032 (Adjusted R Squared = .001)

the frog. Whatever the difference in habitat use that explained intersexual differences in prey size also explained the absence of any prey size differences between males and juveniles.

At the species level, the Cuban treefrog was gram for gram a more aggressive predator of large prey than its competitors on buildings (fig. 9.9; tables 9.25, 9.26) and in nature (fig. 9.10; tables 9.27, 9.28), which meant that even small Cuban treefrogs were eating larger prey than similar-sized competitors, regardless of location. These figures also indicated that prey size differed more between the Cuban treefrog and its competitors than among its competitors.

Number of prey

A somewhat different story emerged regarding the relationship between predator body size and number of prey. Because of the great difference in body size between male and female Cuban treefrogs, fewer prey were found in the stomachs of males than in females on buildings. In all other instances, although females ate the largest prey, number of prey was simi-

Table 9.20. Parameter estimates in the comparison of maximum prey length and number of prey between male and juvenile Cuban treefrogs from buildings in Everglades National Park.

Dependent Variable	Parameter	B	Std. Error	t	Sig.	95% Confidence Interval	
						Lower Bound	Upper Bound
Prey length	Intercept	1.355	.456	2.973	.004	.444	2.266
	SVL	1.939E-02	.011	1.777	.081	-2.426E-03	4.120E-02
	[Sex=Male]	.249	.193	1.292	.201	-.136	.634
	[Sex=Juvenile]	0a	.	.	.	.	.
No. prey	Intercept	.683	.735	.929	.357	-.787	2.153
	SVL	1.014E-02	.018	.576	.567	-2.505E-02	4.533E-02
	[Sex=Male]	-.445	.311	-1.431	.157	-1.066	.177
	[Sex=Juvenile]	0a	.	.	.	.	.

Dependent variables are ln-transformed.
a This parameter is set to zero because it is redundant.

Table 9.21. Tests of between-subjects effects in the comparison of maximum prey length and number of prey between male and female Cuban treefrogs from nature in Everglades National Park.

Source	Dependent Variable	Type III Sum of Squares	df	Mean Square	F	Sig.
Corrected Model	Prey length	23.002[a]	2	11.501	41.704	.000
	No. prey	3.682[b]	2	1.841	5.292	.006
Intercept	Prey length	13.216	1	13.216	47.923	.000
	No. prey	2.190	1	2.190	6.295	.013
SVL	Prey length	4.626	1	4.626	16.775	.000
	No. prey	.104	1	.104	.299	.585
Sex	Prey length	2.418	1	2.418	8.767	.004
	No. prey	1.265	1	1.265	3.637	.058
Error	Prey length	39.711	144	.276		
	No. prey	50.095	144	.348		
Total	Prey length	1173.443	147			
	No. prey	80.686	147			
Corrected Total	Prey length	62.712	146			
	No. prey	53.777	146			

[a] R Squared = .367 (Adjusted R Squared = .358)
[b] R Squared = .068 (Adjusted R Squared = .056)

Table 9.22. Parameter estimates in the comparison of maximum prey length and number of prey between male and female Cuban treefrogs from nature in Everglades National Park.

Dependent Variable	Parameter	B	Std. Error	t	Sig.	95% Confidence Interval	
						Lower Bound	Upper Bound
Prey length	Intercept	1.821	.281	6.476	.000	1.265	2.376
	SVL	1.645E-02	.004	4.096	.000	8.512E-03	2.439E-02
	[Sex=Male]	-.414	.140	-2.961	.004	-.690	-.138
	[Sex=Female]	0a	.	.	.	.	.
No. prey	Intercept	.507	.316	1.606	.110	-.117	1.131
	SVL	-2.467E-03	.005	-.547	.585	-1.138E-02	6.450E-03
	[Sex=Male]	.299	.157	1.907	.058	-1.090E-02	.610
	[Sex=Female]	0a	.	.	.	.	.

Dependent variables are ln-transformed.
a This parameter is set to zero because it is redundant.

Table 9.23. Tests of between-subjects effects in the comparison of maximum prey length and number of prey between male and juvenile Cuban treefrogs from nature in Everglades National Park.

Source	Dependent Variable	Type III Sum of Squares	df	Mean Square	F	Sig.
Corrected Model	Prey length	.149[a]	2	7.433E-02	.233	.793
	No. prey	1.268[b]	2	.634	1.153	.325
Intercept	Prey length	2.977	1	2.977	9.326	.004
	No. prey	1.186	1	1.186	2.158	.149
SVL	Prey length	.144	1	.144	.451	.505
	No. prey	.565	1	.565	1.027	.317
Sex	Prey length	6.605E-02	1	6.605E-02	.207	.651
	No. prey	1.228	1	1.228	2.234	.142
Error	Prey length	13.726	43	.319		
	No. prey	23.640	43	.550		
Total	Prey length	223.403	46			
	No. prey	43.507	46			
Corrected Total	Prey length	13.875	45			
	No. prey	24.908	45			

Dependent variables are ln-transformed.
[a] R Squared = .011 (Adjusted R Squared = −.035)
[b] R Squared = .051 (Adjusted R Squared = .007)

Table 9.24. Parameter estimates in the comparison of maximum prey length and number of prey between male and juvenile Cuban treefrogs from nature in Everglades National Park.

Dependent Variable	Parameter	B	Std. Error	t	Sig.	95% Confidence Interval	
						Lower Bound	Upper Bound
Prey length	Intercept	2.665	.841	3.167	.003	.968	4.362
	SVL	-1.432E-02	.021	-.672	.505	-5.733E-02	2.869E-02
	[Sex=Male]	.112	.247	.455	.651	-.385	.609
	[Sex=Juvenile]	0a	.	.	.	.	.
No. prey	Intercept	1.476	1.104	1.336	.188	-.751	3.703
	SVL	-2.836E-02	.028	-1.013	.317	-8.480E-02	2.808E-02
	[Sex=Male]	.484	.324	1.495	.142	-.169	1.136
	[Sex=Juvenile]	0a	.	.	.	.	.

Dependent variables are ln-transformed.
[a] This parameter is set to zero because it is redundant.

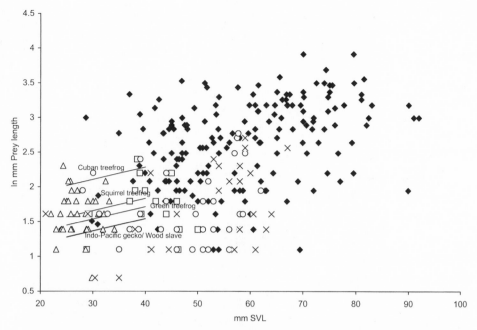

Figure 9.9. Relationship between body size (mm SVL) and maximum prey length (mm) in the Cuban treefrog (diamond), green treefrog (square), squirrel treefrog (triangle), Indo-Pacific gecko (circle), and wood slave (X) from buildings in Everglades National Park. Adjusted means provide regression lines.

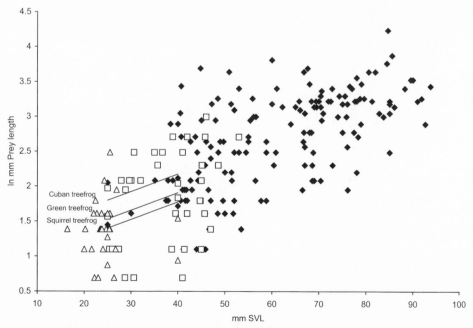

Figure 9.10. Relationship between body size (mm SVL) and maximum prey length (mm) in the Cuban treefrog (diamond), green treefrog (square), and squirrel treefrog (triangle) from natural sites in Everglades National Park. Adjusted means provide regression lines.

Table 9.25. Tests of between-subjects effects in the comparison of maximum prey length and number of prey among the Cuban treefrog, green treefrog, squirrel treefrog, Indo-Pacific gecko, and wood slave from buildings in Everglades National Park.

Source	Dependent Variable	Type III Sum of Squares	df	Mean Square	F	Sig.
Corrected Model	Prey length	73.642a	5	14.728	53.196	.000
	No. prey	57.111b	5	11.422	13.306	.000
Intercept	Prey length	21.558	1	21.558	77.861	.000
	No. prey	26.095	1	26.095	30.399	.000
SVL	Prey length	13.600	1	13.600	49.121	.000
	No. prey	.904	1	.904	1.053	.306
Species	Prey length	24.654	4	6.163	22.261	.000
	No. prey	43.458	4	10.865	12.657	.000
Error	Prey length	80.016	289	.277		
	No. prey	248.083	289	.858		
Total	Prey length	1639.966	295			
	No. prey	641.507	295			
Corrected Total	Prey length	153.658	294			
	No. prey	305.193	294			

Dependent variables are ln-transformed.
a R Squared = .479 (Adjusted R Squared = .470)
b R Squared = .187 (Adjusted R Squared = .173)

Table 9.26. Parameter estimates in the comparison of maximum prey length and number of prey among the Cuban treefrog (CTF), green treefrog (GTF), squirrel treefrog (STF), Indo-Pacific gecko (IPG), and wood slave (WS) from buildings in Everglades National Park.

Dependent Variable	Parameter	B	Std. Error	t	Sig.	95% Confidence Interval	
						Lower Bound	Upper Bound
Prey length	Intercept	.831	.161	5.162	.000	.514	1.148
	SVL	1.780E-02	.003	7.009	.000	1.280E-02	2.280E-02
	[Species=CTF]	.740	.109	6.806	.000	.526	.954
	[Species=GTF]	.170	.170	.998	.319	-.165	.504
	[Species=STF]	.290	.145	2.003	.046	5.039E-03	.576
	[Species=IPG]	-3.315E-03	.134	-.025	.980	-.266	.259
	[Species=WS]	0a	.	.	.	.	.
No. prey	Intercept	.777	.283	2.743	.006	.220	1.335
	SVL	4.588E-03	.004	1.026	.306	-4.214E-03	1.339E-02
	[Species=CTF]	-.210	.191	-1.098	.273	-.587	.167
	[Species=GTF]	1.152	.299	3.850	.000	.563	1.742
	[Species=STF]	1.078	.255	4.224	.000	.576	1.580
	[Species=IPG]	-1.948E-02	.235	-.083	.934	-.482	.443
	[Species=WS]	0a	.	.	.	.	.

[a] This parameter is set to zero because it is redundant.

Table 9.27. Test of between-subjects effects in the comparison of maximum prey length and number of prey among the Cuban treefrog, green treefrog, and squirrel treefrog from nature in Everglades National Park.

Source	Dependent Variable	Type III Sum of Squares	df	Mean Square	F	Sig.
Corrected Model	Prey length	78.094[a]	3	26.031	87.355	0
	No. prey	42.686[b]	3	14.229	24.978	.000
Intercept	Prey length	18.123	1	18.123	60.816	.000
	No. prey	33.580	1	33.580	58.950	.000
SVL	Prey length	25.678	1	25.678	86.171	.000
	No. prey	2.959	1	2.959	5.195	.024
Species	Prey length	2.390	2	1.195	4.010	.020
	No. prey	15.644	2	7.822	13.731	.000
Error	Prey length	62.877	211	.298		
	No. prey	120.193	211	.570		
Total	Prey length	1399.182	215			
	No. prey	245.535	215			
Corrected Total	Prey length	140.971	214			
	No. prey	162.879	214			

[a] R Squared = .554 (Adjusted R Squared = .548)
[b] R Squared = .262 (Adjusted R Squared = .252)

Table 9.28. Parameter estimates in the comparison of maximum prey length and number of prey among the Cuban treefrog (CTF), green treefrog (GTF), squirrel treefrog (STF), Indo-Pacific gecko (IPG), and wood slave (WS) from nature in Everglades National Park.

Dependent Variable	Parameter	B	Std. Error	t	Sig.	95% Confidence Interval	
						Lower Bound	Upper Bound
Prey length	Intercept	.773	.125	6.201	.000	.527	1.019
	SVL	2.512E-02	.003	9.283	.000	1.979E-02	3.046E-02
	[Species=CTF]	.398	.154	2.580	.011	9.392E-02	.702
	[Species=GTF]	.131	.148	.884	.378	-.161	.424
	[Species=STF]	0	.	.	.	.	.
No. prey	Intercept	1.962	.172	11.379	.000	1.622	2.301
	SVL	-8.528E-03	.004	-2.279	.024	-1.590E-02	-1.153E-03
	[Species=CTF]	-1.013	.213	-4.750	.000	-1.433	-.593
	[Species=GTF]	-.994	.205	-4.843	.000	-1.399	-.589
	[Species=STF]	0	.	.	.	.	.

[a] This parameter is set to zero because it is redundant.

lar or smaller between size-classes and sexes of the Cuban treefrog. On the other hand, its competitors, all of which ate smaller prey, also ate as many or more prey than did the Cuban treefrog (table 9.16). Both hylids, for example, ate more prey than the Cuban treefrog. A Cuban treefrog might eat two or three large roaches, but I recorded a squirrel treefrog with 76 flies in its gut! Both geckos ate similar numbers of prey as the Cuban treefrog, perhaps because their diet included slightly larger prey than that of the native treefrogs. The equivocal pattern of prey numbers among species was reflected in the absence of any significant relationship between predator body size and number of prey for any of the five species (fig. 9.11–9.15). The relationship between number of prey and maximum prey length was significant for only the squirrel treefrog and the Indo-Pacific gecko (fig. 9.16–9.20).

As in the case of maximum prey length, I wanted to know what role, if any, body size of the predator played in the number of prey eaten by these five species in the park. The ANCOVA revealed that among Cuban treefrogs no body size or gender effects existed for number of prey on buildings, either between males and females (fig. 9.21; table 9.17, 9.18) or

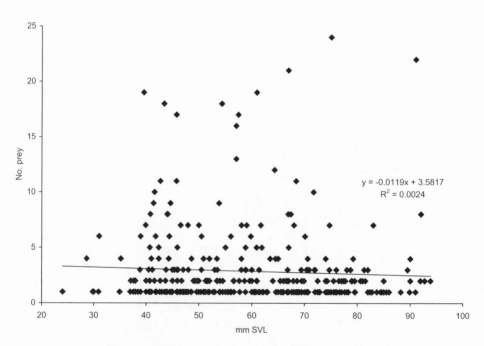

Figure 9.11. Relationship between body size (mm SVL) and number of prey in the Cuban treefrog from Everglades National Park. F = 0.8187, P > 0.05.

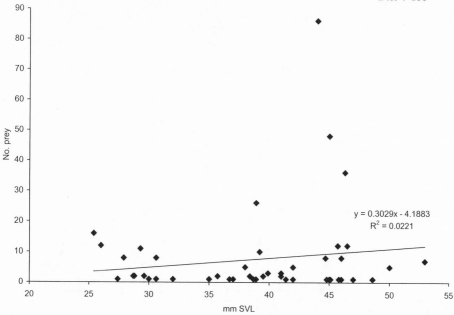

Figure 9.12. Relationship between body size (mm SVL) and number of prey in the green treefrog from Everglades National Park. F = 1.038, p > 0.05.

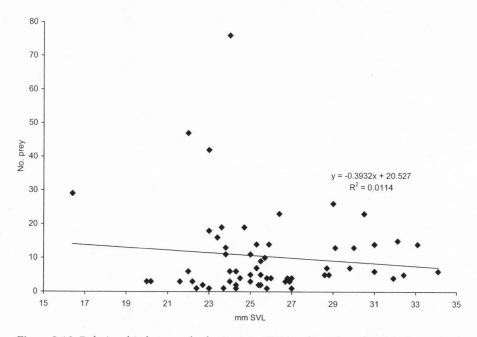

Figure 9.13. Relationship between body size (mm SVL) and number of prey in the squirrel treefrog from Everglades National Park. F = 0.682, p > 0.5.

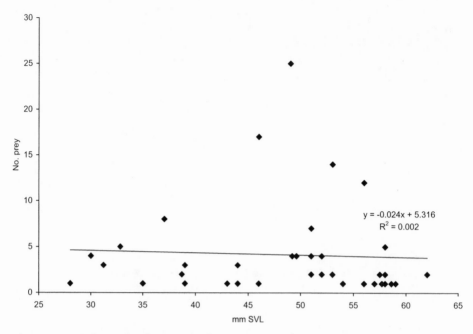

Figure 9.14. Relationship between body size (mm SVL) and number of prey in the Indo-Pacific gecko from Everglades National Park. $F = 0.0710$, $p > 0.05$.

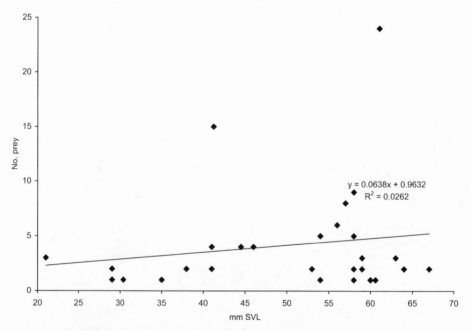

Figure 9.15. Relationship between body size (mm SVL) and number of prey in the wood slave from Everglades National Park. $F = 0.701$, $p > 0.05$.

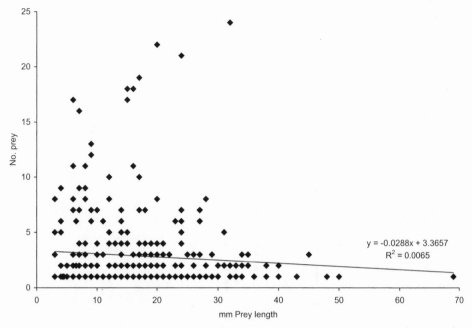

Figure 9.16. Relationship between maximum prey length (mm) and number of prey in the Cuban treefrog from Everglades National Park. F = 1.956, p > 0.05.

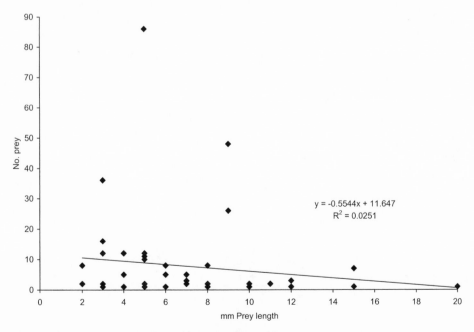

Figure 9.17. Relationship between maximum prey length (mm) and number of prey in the green treefrog from Everglades National Park. F = 1.182, p > 0.05.

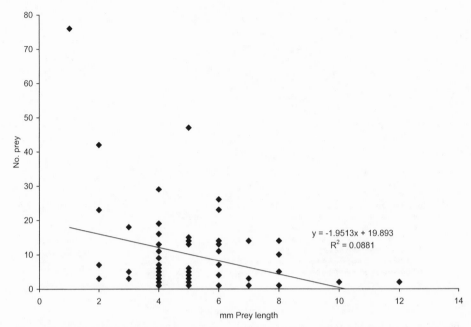

Figure 9.18. Relationship between maximum prey length (mm) and number of prey in the squirrel treefrog from Everglades National Park. $F = 5.704$, $p < 0.02$.

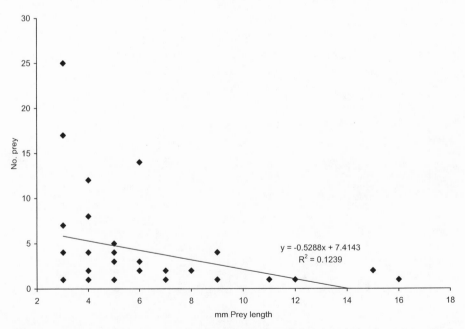

Figure 9.19. Relationship between maximum prey length (mm) and number of prey in the Indo-Pacific gecko from Everglades National Park. $F = 5.090$, $p < 0.03$.

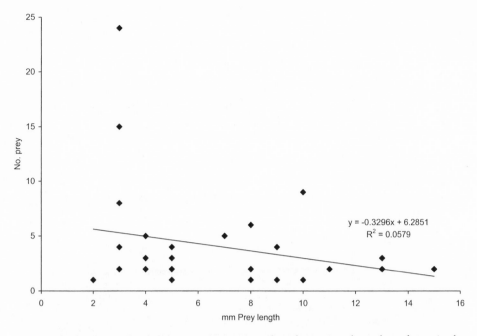

Figure 9.20. Relationship between maximum prey length (mm) and number of prey in the wood slave from Everglades National Park. $F = 1.60$, $P > 0.05$.

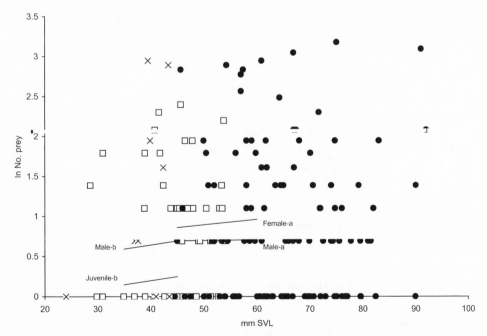

Figure 9.21. Relationship between body size (mm SVL) and number of prey in male (square), female (circle), and juvenile (X) Cuban treefrogs from buildings in Everglades National Park. Adjusted means provide regression lines.

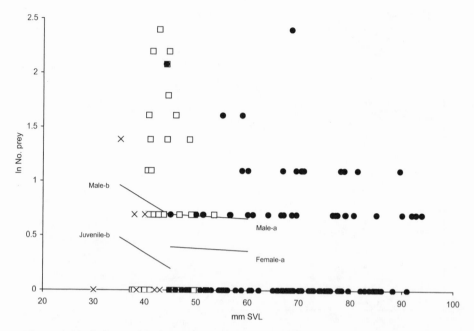

Figure 9.22. Relationship between body size (mm SVL) and number of prey in male (square), female (circle), and juvenile (X) Cuban treefrogs from natural sites in Everglades National Park. Adjusted means provide regression lines.

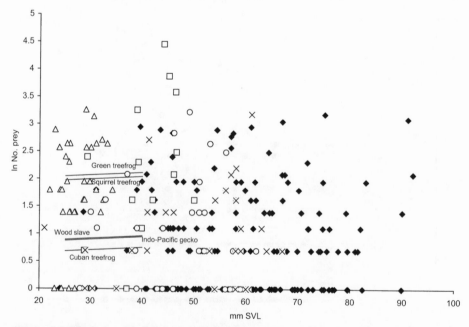

Figure 9.23. Relationship between body size (mm SVL) and number of prey in the Cuban treefrog (diamond), green treefrog (square), squirrel treefrog (triangle), Indo-Pacific gecko (circle), and wood slave (X) from buildings in Everglades National Park. Adjusted means provide regression lines.

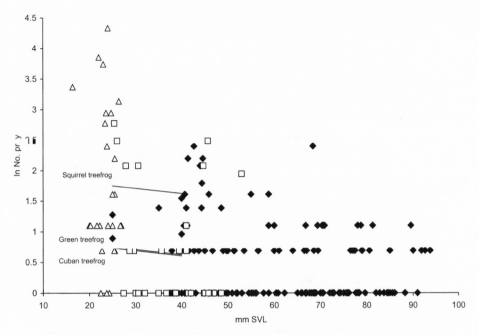

Figure 9.24. Relationship between body size (mm SVL) and number of prey in the Cuban treefrog (diamond), green treefrog (square), and squirrel treefrog (triangle) from natural sites in Everglades National Park. Adjusted means provide regression lines.

between males and juveniles (fig. 9.21; tables 9.19, 9.20). In nature, number of prey eaten was also similar between males and females (fig. 9.22; tables 9.21, 9.22) and between males and juveniles (fig. 9.22; tables 9.23, 9.24), which meant that no one segment of the Cuban treefrog population ate any more or any less prey than other segments of the population.

The ANCOVA also revealed that the Cuban treefrog ate fewer prey than its competitors on buildings (fig. 9.23; tables 9.25, 9.26) and that, in nature (fig. 9.24; tables 9.27, 9.28), more prey were eaten by the squirrel treefrog than by either the Cuban treefrog or the green treefrog. This finding confirms that the Cuban treefrog ate larger but nearly always fewer prey than its potential competitors.

Vertebrates in the diet

Clearly, the trophic reward for large body size in the Cuban treefrog was the ability to eat large-bodied prey. Not only did the Cuban treefrog eat larger individuals of the same prey taxa as its competitors, but it also ate vertebrates, *including* its competitors. Most of the vertebrates eaten in the park were anurans: six species of anurans (N = 41), including conspecifics, were eaten by 40 Cuban treefrogs (table 9.29). Thirty-six of the batrachophagous individuals were female, and no batrachophagous juveniles were found. Thus, batrachophagy was recorded from 3.6 percent of the males and 12.4 percent of the females examined in the study, or 10.0 percent of all adults examined. The predator (68.1 ± 12.1 mm SVL; 40–90; N = 35) was on average 2.6X the body length of its prey (25.9 ± 7.6 mm SVL; 10–45; N = 35), and large Cuban treefrogs ate increasingly large anurans (r = 0.62, P < 0.00, N = 35). Treefrogs were the most frequently eaten category of anurans by the Cuban treefrog and for the longest part of the year (table 9.29). Incidence of batrachophagy was highest at a slough where the abundance of hylids was high and the population of Cuban treefrogs comprised almost exclusively, for reasons that were unclear, large-bodied females.

The findings in chapter 8 revealed the predictability and severity of a Cuban treefrog-native treefrog interaction, which had more to do with predation than competition for food. Behavioral interactions suggested that neither prey species recognized the Cuban treefrog as a predator. For example, on lighted portions of buildings in the Everglades and southern Florida, hylids foraged alongside Cuban treefrogs, including those large enough to be dangerous. Also, occasionally all three species shared diurnal retreats in which individuals of both species were in direct contact with Cuban treefrogs. Moreover, the native treefrogs are small and not chemically or structurally protected from the depredations of the Cuban treefrog.

The second most frequently eaten anuran was the eastern narrowmouth toad, *Gastrophryne carolinensis* (table 9.29). This species was seasonally exploited near buildings where individuals were visible in the short grass and pavement above which Cuban treefrogs perched and looked down in wait of prey. Predation on the eastern narrowmouth toad was recorded during July–November when conditions were wettest and above-ground activity was great on the part of both predator and prey. The narrowmouth toad, the smallest anuran species eaten by the Cuban treefrog, was also the only species recorded in males. Conspecifics were eaten infrequently (table 9.29). One leopard frog, *Rana sphenocephala* (24.0 mm SVL), and one southern toad, *Bufo terrestris* (30.2 mm SVL), were also consumed from natural areas during the wet season.

The Indo-Pacific gecko was a sit-and-wait forager on buildings but moved around a lot in the course of the night. Individuals were stationary

Table 9.29. Anurans in the diet of the Cuban treefrog from Everglades National Park.

Month	Cuban treefrog	Green treefrog	Squirrel treefrog	Hylidae	Leopard frog	Southern toad	Eastern narrow-mouth toad	Total	% Total
Jan	0	0	0	0	0	0	0	0	0.0
Feb	0	0	0	0	0	0	0	0	0.0
Mar	0	1	0	0	0	0	0	1	2.4
Apr	0	1	0	0	0	0	0	1	2.4
May	0	0	1	0	0	0	0	1	2.4
Jun	0	0	4	0	1	1	0	6	14.6
Jul	0	1	0	0	0	0	1	2	4.9
Aug	1	0	2	1	0	0	1	5	12.2
Sep	0	2	1	0	0	0	1	4	9.8
Oct	2	3	5	0	0	0	1	11	26.9
Nov	0	1	0	1	0	0	3	5	12.2
Dec	0	3	0	2	0	0	0	5	12.2
Total	3	12	13	4	1	1	7	41	100.0
% Total	7.3	29.2	31.7	9.8	2.4	2.4	17.1		

when near lights, but this gecko was never observed feeding alongside its predator. Individuals were easily startled by movements and responded by running to the nearest refuge, even if a few meters away. In spite of that, the remains of an individual were recovered from the stomach of a building-dwelling Cuban treefrog. The very fresh remains of a single wood slave came from a female found staring at a screen that was traversed by geckos on Fish Hut, where the wood slave was the more abundant gecko. A single brown anole (*Anolis sagrei*) came from a boardwalk. It remains to be seen if geckos are differentially susceptible to predation by the Cuban treefrog. For example, when captured by hand, the wood slave bit and struggled more forcefully than the Indo-Pacific gecko. If those behaviors interfere with predation success, the wood slave could have a competitive edge over the Indo-Pacific gecko when in sympatry with the Cuban treefrog.

Cannibalism among postmetamorphic Cuban treefrogs occurs at other sites. A large female from Okeechobee was found to contain two freshly ingested fertile males, and a female from Tampa was found with a freshly ingested brown anole (Meshaka 1996c). Elsewhere in the Caribbean, the Cuban treefrog eats the brown anole, the greenhouse frog (*Eleutherodactylus planirostris planirostris*), and the eastern narrowmouth toad (Meshaka 1996g).

Inclusion of vertebrates in the diet is common among the exotic herpetofauna of Florida (Meshaka et al. 2001) and indicative of a broad diet. Some of the species that eat vertebrates are omnivorous, such as the Cuban knight anole (*Anolis equestris equestris*), the Cuban green anole (*A. porcatus*), the Mexican spinytail iguana (*Ctenosaura pectinata*), the Central American spinytail iguana (*C. similis*), the northern curlytail lizard (*Leiocephalus carinatus armouri*), and the marine toad (*Bufo marinus*). Other vertebrate-eaters, like the Cuban treefrog, are primarily insectivorous, such as the brown anole, brown basilisk (*Basiliscus vittatus*), and tokay gecko (*Gekko gecko*). At least one exotic species, the spectacled caiman (*Caiman crocodylus*), is carnivorous (Meshaka et al. 2001).

In the West Indies, the marine toad, leopard frog, bullfrog (*R. catesbeiana*), and pig frog (*R. grylio*) are all exotic (Schwartz and Henderson 1991), and, like the native *O. dominicensis,* include vertebrates in their diets (Carr 1940; Duellman and Schwartz 1958; Rossi 1981; Duer et al. 1993).

Foraging behavior

The Cuban treefrog was mostly, if not exclusively, a sit-and-wait predator. I observed individuals hunting prey from the ground to the tops of trees; they nearly always ambushed their prey from above, usually from less than 60 cm. For example, individuals stared from the curb at the road surface 10 cm beneath them or at the ground from an air conditioner, a pipe, or a wall. In nature, individuals stared from one branch to a lower branch in front of them or stared at the ground from the trunk of a tree. Occasionally individuals hunted along the same surface where they were perched; for example, capturing prey that traversed their view on a sidewalk, and the same strategy was used on broad horizontal limbs of trees. Lastly, individuals stared at structures up to one meter away, directly in front of them, and awaited movement. On buildings, individuals perched near the tops of drainpipes or limbs of adjacent trees and stared at a lighted wall where they caught light-attracted prey on building walls and then quickly returned to their perches. Similarly in nature, the Cuban treefrog perched on horizontal limbs above the ground and stared at ones nearby.

With the exception of an *en masse* dispersal event up a wall that I observed at Anhinga Trail, metamorphoslings were occasionally observed from ground level up to approximately one meter above the ground in an alert posture at night. Females perched in hunting postures from as low as the ground to approximately 10 m in the tops of trees, their large body size making it easy to spot and sex them as they perched crosswise on high limbs. Like females and juveniles, males were observed hunting from the ground. They were also seen with certainty up to three meters above the ground in trees, and were heard calling on occasion a meter or so above that.

The difficulty in spotting a small lichenate-patterned frog in a tree hinders unqualified statements about intraspecific differences in perch heights of this species. Clearly, at night this species was probably safer from predators when high above the ground despite a larger prey base near the ground, and females were best able to exploit larger prey found at those heights, such as large roaches routinely seen climbing up trees at night. It is also a fair argument to say that males were also up in the trees and just unable to capture the large roaches. Lastly, perch height differences between the sexes based on diet were evident: the preponderance of spiders in the stomachs of males, the overwhelming presence of spiders near the ground, and the fact that spiders were not exploited much by females despite their having exploited other small prey. These considerations lead me to think that despite great overlap in habitat use between sexes and size-classes, there was probably a measure of biologically meaningful difference in perching heights, probably body-size-dependent more than simply a sexual difference, in the Cuban treefrog. This would explain a relatively high degree of dietary overlap within the species, with some notable differences in the frequencies of some prey taxa. For its competitors, this meant that predaceous individuals and potential competitors were everywhere. With the exception of the knight anole, which clearly searches out live prey in tree cavities and palm thatching (Meshaka et al. 2001), all of the anoles, geckos, and the marine toad sit and wait for their prey.

Prey capture

The Cuban treefrog ate a lot of roaches and frogs, especially treefrogs. Observations on prey capture and ingestion help explain the frequency of these prey in its diet.

In nature, roaches, being the most numerous prey item in the highest number of stomachs of females, were captured most often by an overhead ambush, but also by a frontal attack. Chemically protected roaches, like the Florida stinking roach (*Eurycotus* sp.), were usually swallowed quickly headfirst. Struggling Florida stinking roaches, able to chemically defend themselves, were held with their posterior end hanging out of the mouth of their predator. The Cuban treefrogs dragged the roaches backwards for a few centimeters, thereby wiping the toxin onto the substrate, then engulfed the entire roach. The sequence was repeated if the taste was still unacceptable. For a few minutes after ingestion, Cuban treefrogs sat with mouths open and wiped their mouths with their forefeet. Individuals in these circumstances were also seen in the field on a few occasions.

In chapter 8, I noted a negative association between abundances of the Cuban treefrog and the two native hylid treefrogs. I also noted in this chapter that the hylids did not behave in ways that suggested they recognize the Cuban treefrog as their predator. Naïveté by the hylids toward their predator was especially detrimental: native hylid treefrogs never stood a chance in captive encounters with their competitor/predator. The Cuban treefrog was generally accurate on an attack, and handling time for all but the largest green treefrogs was less than one minute. This basically meant that the Cuban treefrog needed only to find a treefrog in order to successfully eat it. Presumably, the likelihood of this happening was greatest on the bare walls of buildings, which provided little if any cover.

On the other hand, even small conspecifics responded quite a bit differently to a predatory attack by the Cuban treefrog. Once grabbed, the attacked conspecific kicked furiously. A head grab, which was the only way to eat a conspecific, was met by forearms locked at 90-degree angles outside of the predator's mouth, effectively preventing ingestion of all but the smallest individuals. Consequently, although the threat of cannibalism is high enough to enforce body size-pairing of resting individuals (Meshaka 1996b), cannibalism in this species was difficult to accomplish.

10

Predation

Predators

The Cuban treefrog has faced many predator species in the southern Everglades (table 10.1), yet predator pressure has not seemed to affect its success in establishing viable populations in this area. For one thing, in the park none of its predators specialize in treefrogs or tadpoles, even if both life stages are included in the diet (table 10.2). A second reason for its success, despite high predator diversity in the park, is that few predators are found in all habitats occupied by the Cuban treefrog (table 10.3). Body size is also an advantage in decreasing predator pressure. Large body size, especially in females, restricted some predators, like the ribbon snake (*Thamnophis sauritus*), to juvenile Cuban treefrogs, and protected the largest individuals from other predators like the racer (*Coluber constrictor*). Lastly, most predators were subject to interguild predation; besides removing Cuban treefrogs from the population, they were also removing one another.

The fewest predators resided around buildings in the park. By extension, very few predators of the Cuban treefrog, whether native or exotic, were found in disturbed habitats anywhere in Florida. Therefore, disturbed systems, the Cuban treefrog's ever-expanding habitat in Florida, came closest among the habitats studied to approaching a predator-free state. However, even around buildings in towns and cities, invertebrate predators fed on tadpoles, and assorted vertebrates, like grackles (*Quiscalus quiscula*), barn owls (*Tyto alba*), racers (Meshaka and Ferster 1995), and garter snakes (*Thamnophis sirtalis*) (Meshaka and Jansen 1997), captured postmetamorphic individuals.

The Cuban treefrog will encounter few new predator species in north Florida and will lose none of its southern Florida predators. Consequently,

Table 10.1. Predators of the Cuban treefrog in Everglades National Park.

Species	Field observations	Field trials	Captive trials
Amphibia			
Hylidae			
Osteopilus septentrionalis	X	X	
Reptilia			
Chelydridae			
Chelyda serpentina		X	
Colubridae			
Coluber constrictor	X[1]		
Elaphe guttata	X		
E. obsoleta	X[1]		
Nerodia fasciata		X	X
Thamnophis sauritus	X[2]		
T. sirtalis	X[3]	X	X
Viperidae			
Agkistrodon piscivorus	X	X	X
Aves			
Ardeidae			
Egretta caerulea	X		
Corvidae			
Corvus brachyrynchus	X	X	
Strigidae			
Strix varia		X[4]	
Tytonidae			
Tyto alba	X		

[1] Meshaka and Ferster, 1995.
[2] Love, 1995.
[3] Meshaka and Jansen, 1997.
[4] Meshaka, 1996.

predator pressure will be no more of a barrier to establishment in the southeastern coastal plain than it has been in southern Florida.

Seven forms were confirmed to be predators of the Cuban treefrog in Cuba (table 10.4). Like those of Florida, most of its predators were ophidian. Interestingly, two of its predators in Cuba, the knight anole (*Anolis equestris equestris*) and the barn owl, are also predators of the Cuban treefrog in southern Florida. The former species, although not established in the Everglades, has been reported on Long Pine Key and is ubiquitous in urban areas of extreme southern Florida (Meshaka et al. 2000, 2001).

Among the few exotic amphibians and reptiles that have received some attention, most are subject to high numbers of predators (Meshaka et al.

Table 10.2. Predators of larval and post-metamorphic Cuban treefrogs in the southern Everglades and Everglades National Park.

Species	Tadpoles	Post-metamorphic individuals	Total
Amphibia			
Hylidae			
Osteopilus septentrionalis		X	1
Reptilia			
Chelydridae			
Chelydra serpentina	X	X	2
Colubridae			
Coluber constrictor		X	1
Elaphe guttata		X	1
E. obsoleta		X	1
Nerodia fasciata	X	X	2
Thamnophis sauritus	X	X	2
T. sirtalis		X	1
Viperidae			
Agkistrodon piscivorus		X	1
Aves			
Ardeidae			
Egretta caerulea	X	X	2
Corvidae			
Corvus brachyrynchus		X	1
Passeridae			
Quiscalus quiscula		X	1
Strigidae			
Strix varia		X	1
Tytonidae			
Tyto alba		X	1
Total	4	14	

2001). Interestingly, the brown anole (*Anolis sagrei*), subject to the most predators (both native and exotic) is, like the Cuban treefrog, also among the most successful. The greenhouse frog (*Eleutherodactylus planirostris planirostris*) has numerous predators, and is also found in more Florida counties than the Cuban treefrog (Meshaka et al. 2001). Other factors can play a greater role in shaping ranges of introduced species than predator pressure. For example, the marine toad (*Bufo marinus*), another successful colonizer of Florida and elsewhere, has very few confirmed predators in Florida, yet remains confined to southern and coastal Florida.

Table 10.3. Predators of the Cuban treefrog and the habitats in which they have been observed in Everglades National Park.

Species	Pineland	Tropical hammock	Mangrove	Coastal prairie pond	Slough	Marsh	Prairie	Disturbed	Building	Total
Reptilia										
Chelydridae										
Chelydra serpentina					X					1
Colubridae										
Coluber constrictor	X	X		X			X	X	X	6
Elaphe guttata	X	X	X	X			X	X	X	7
E. obsoleta	X	X	X	X			X	X	X	7
Nerodia fasciata					X	X	X			3
Thamnophis sauritus				X			X	X		3
T. sirtalis		X		X			X	X	X	5
Viperidae										
Agkistrodon piscivorus	X						X			2
Aves										
Ardeidae										
Egretta caerulea				X		X	X			3
Corvidae										
Corvus brachyrynchus	X		X						X	3
Strigidae										
Strix varia		X			X	X	X			4
Tytonidae										
Tyto alba			X	X					X	3
Total	5	5	4	7	3	3	9	5	6	

Table 10.4. West Indian predators of the Cuban treefrog.

Species	Cuba	Bahamas	Cayman Islands	United States	Total
Boidae					
Epicrates striatus[2]		X	X		2
Tropidophis canus[3]		X			1
T. caymanensis[3]			X		1
T. melanurus[3,4]	X				1
T. pardalis[4]	X				1
Colubridae					
Alsophis cantherigerus[4,5]	X				1
A. vudii[3]		X			1
Antillophis spp.[4]	X				1
Arhyton spp.[4]	X				1
Iguanidae					
Anolis equestris[6,7]	X			X	2
Aves					
Tytonidae					
Tyto alba[8]	X	X	X	X	4
Total	7	4	3	2	

[1] Meshaka, 1994a.
[2] Franz et al., 1993.
[3] Schwartz and Henderson, 1991.
[4] Luis Moreno, pers. commun.
[5] William B. Robertson, Jr., pers. commun.
[6] Barbour and Ramsden, 1919.
[7] Brach, 1976.
[8] This study.

Injuries

Injured Cuban treefrogs were rare in collections from the Everglades. From a sample of 2,151 individuals, only three males (38.7, 50.1, and 54.5 mm SVL) and nine females (68.1 ± 13.0 mm SVL; range = 52.4–93.8) showed signs of external injury. Three of the injured individuals (93.8, 84.5, and 55.8 mm SVL) were found in natural systems. Of those three individuals, two were the largest in the entire sample of injured Cuban treefrogs. Sustaining past injuries, individuals were found without part or all of the rear left leg (N = 5), rear right leg (N = 4), and left hand (N = 1). Three individuals were caught with fresh wounds. A female (70.5 mm SVL) was found bleeding from a puncture wound on her head. Two other females (59.8 and 55.8 mm SVL) were found with incisions running lengthwise down their backs. The smaller of these two individuals was also found with her front right leg ripped almost completely off at the shoulder.

Urban Cuban treefrogs also sustained wounds. One morning in June 1998, a large (> 80 mm SVL) female was found hiding in the axil of a bromeliad in the front yard of my residence. She had a fresh V-shaped bite mark on her head and an open wound on her back from which approximately 5 mm of entrails protruded. I believe she was attacked by a knight anole, a species also present in my yard. The next morning she was found resting in the filter trap of the swimming pool behind the house. She returned to the filter trap periodically, and within two weeks her wound had healed.

Antipredator behavior

The Cuban treefrog was not an easy frog to capture or to eat. Its primary defense was to avoid detection. Resting Cuban treefrogs, and especially small individuals, wedged into folds (e.g., palm boots, roof shingles), and large ones often packed into cavities, such as tree cavities or pipes (Meshaka 1996b). A Cuban treefrog that was backed into a confining refuge faced its attacker. When threatened, Cuban treefrogs of all sizes worked themselves as far back into the retreat as possible, dropped their heads to an oblique angle, and closed their eyes. In this position, a Cuban treefrog's head phragmotically provided a bony seal that could obstruct a grab by a snake and also provided a stony shield against abuse. Cuban treefrogs grabbed by garter snakes and yellow rat snakes (*Elaphe obsoleta quadrivittata*) kicked furiously, swelled with air in 3 to 4 gulps, screamed, and exuded a pungent, sticky, viscous substance. If grabbed by its head, the Cuban treefrog locked its arms in 90-degree angles to further inhibit ingestion.

These defenses make large Cuban treefrogs difficult to be held and eaten. A snake would have a difficult time holding onto and extracting a Cuban treefrog from a cavity through a small aperture. Predators that capture a Cuban treefrog outside of a refuge are faced with a large, kicking, sticky mess. With the possible exception of its chemical defense, these secondary defenses employed by the Cuban treefrog seemed tailor-made to repel the primarily ophidian suite of predators, both in Florida and in the West Indies.

To avoid avian predators, the Cuban treefrog simply had to avoid extraction by its choice of refuges, or avoid detection while out and about by cryptic coloration. An active Cuban treefrog, lichenate in pattern, blended very well with many kinds of tree bark. Its leg bands connected when the frog was sitting and obscured the form of its body. Activity was curtailed on moonlit nights, when a cast shadow might give away its presence to a sight-oriented predator. The Cuban treefrog was skittish if active on such nights and any movements caused an abrupt end to calling. Individuals either crouched flat and remained immobile for a while, climbed away quickly, or hopped far into bushes.

After watching depredation by birds in staged and natural encounters, I understood why the Cuban treefrog behaved the way it did. Once captured by a bird, the Cuban treefrog scarcely stood a chance. Even large individuals that carelessly rested in semi-exposed situations, such as under awnings, were pulled from their ledges by crows, taken to open areas, deflated, flung around, and eviscerated very easily. Common grackles were also adept at this. Barn owls grabbed Cuban treefrogs from roads, and barred owls also ate them, even if they had first to dance around them with open wings to block a retreat (Meshaka 1996e).

Mammalian predators may well be the object of its chemical defense, which produces a burning, itching sensation to mucous membranes for up to 20 minutes (*pers. obs.*). The toxin was also aromatic in closed quarters (*pers. obs.*). Perhaps the Cuban treefrog's chemical defense originated in a neotropical progenitor that contended with an array of arboreal mammalian predators. That being the case, its success in Florida, where it crossed faunistic boundaries, may have been a replay of its biogeographic history in the West Indies. If this is true, the present-day distribution of the Cuban treefrog in Cuba and the Bahamas may also have been facilitated by a dearth of mammalian predators and an ability to sufficiently defend itself against an array of ophidian and avian predators as one sees today.

Regardless of the primary selective agent for chemical defense in the Cuban treefrog, chemical protection is predicted to secondarily insulate the Cuban treefrog from many nontraditional predators, as it does for the marine toad in its introduced range (Krakauer 1968; Rossi 1981).

Body Size

Body size, body size-dimorphism, and abundance of the Cuban treefrog

How big are Cuban treefrogs, and what accounts for their body size? Across its geographic range, male Cuban treefrogs matured at surprisingly small body sizes of about 28 mm SVL and, as adults, remained smaller on average than females (table 5.21). Although averaging 45 to 50 mm SVL as adults, fertile males (those with enlarged testes and nuptial pads), were generally larger than sexually quiescent males (table 5.21), and they mated with increasingly large-bodied females.

In the park, adult body size varied among sites, more so among females than among males (fig. 11.1). The significant intersite variation in body size was best explained by abundance. Crowded sites were predictably characterized by the presence of small-bodied females, and large-bodied females were found in small populations. Males, on the other hand, increased slightly but not significantly in body size as population size increased. Consequently, degree of sexual dimorphism in body size of this species in the park was dictated by variation in the body size of the female.

Intraspecific competition is one explanation for the density-dependent component of body size observed in females. If so, females may have achieved a minimum body size beyond which when crowded they competed with one another for food. The result was many stunted females, as recorded from heavily populated buildings. Males, on the other hand, having called throughout the year and living barely past one year, may simply never have eaten enough food or lived long enough to grow to that critical minimum size. If true, there would be no reason to expect males to decrease in body size when crowded. In fact, an opposite pattern was suggested when I compared body size of males to their abundance (figure 11.1). The finding of slight, even if not significant, increase in body size

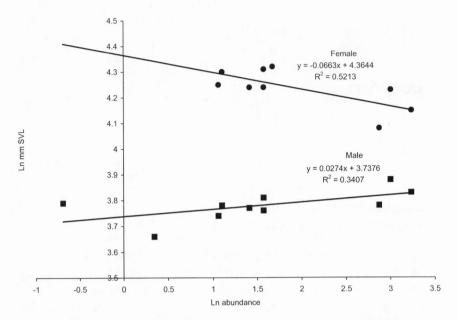

Figure 11.1. Relationship of body size and abundance in male (square) and female (circle) Cuban treefrogs from Everglades National Park. (Females, F = 7.50, p < 0.03; Males, p > 0.05).

associated with abundance suggests an effect of intraspecific competition, whereby males were small where they were scarce because they died earlier than their numerous counterparts on buildings that were not yet crowded enough to compete.

On a broader scale, males likewise did not vary in mean adult body size (ANOVA; F = 0.592, N = 398, df = 29, $P > 0.05$), whereas females did (ANOVA; F = 6.058, N = 468, df = 30, $P < 0.000$) from a wide range of sites sampled across native and introduced geographic ranges of the Cuban treefrog. The idea that ecology enforces small body size in male Cuban treefrogs is tested by the few giant males in collections (Meshaka 1996f). In at least one case, the Florida male was alone or nearly so and lived on the buildings of a shade-cloth nursery probably for several years.

Body size of nearest relatives

Compared with its nearest relatives, the Cuban treefrog is a giant species (table 11.1). It is the largest hylid treefrog in Florida and, for that matter, all of North America (Conant and Collins 1991). In the southern Ever-

Table 11.1. Maximum body sizes (mm SVL) of hylid treefrogs of the Everglades and West Indies.

Site	Sex		
	Male	Female	Unknown
Everglades			
Acris gryllus dorsalis[1]			25
Hyla cinerea[1]			64
H. gratiosa[1]			70
H. squirella[1]			41
Pseudacris nigrita verrucosa[1]			32
P. ocularis[1]			17
West Indies			
Calyptohyla crucialis[2]		122	
H. heilprini[2]		52	
H. marianae[2]		40	
H. pulchrilineata[2]		43	
H. vasta[2]	109	142	
H. wilderi[2]		29	
Osteopilus brunneus[2]	51	76	
O. dominicensis[3]	80	100	
O. septentrionalis[4,5]	112	165	

[1] Conant and Collins, 1991.
[2] Schwartz and Henderson, 1991.
[3] This study.
[4] Mittleman, 1950b.
[5] Meshaka, 1996f.

glades, the Cuban treefrog co-occurs with a medium-sized treefrog, the green treefrog (*Hyla cinerea*) and a small-bodied treefrog, the squirrel treefrog (*Hyla squirella*). In Puerto Rico and Hawaii, where it is exotic, the Cuban treefrog is the only treefrog. In its native range, the Cuban treefrog co-occurs with no other native treefrog.

In Jamaica, body size-pairing exists among the hylids with small (*Hyla marianae* and *H. wilderi*), medium (*O. brunneus*), and large (*Calyptohyla crucialis*) species, but the Cuban treefrog is larger than all of them (table 11.1). Likewise, on Hispaniola, small (*H. heilprini* and *H. pulchrilineata*), medium (*O. dominicensis*), and large (*H. vasta*) species co-occur, but are smaller than the Cuban treefrog (table 11.1). Interestingly, the Cuban treefrog's congeners are not the largest hylids on those islands. Large body size, although advantageous to a colonizing animal for several reasons, does not by itself explain the small geographic range and poor colonizing ability of other West Indian hylids. Body size notwithstanding, all the Jamaican forms require bromeliads for breeding (Schwartz and Henderson 1991), which doubtless restricts their colonizing abilities. Among the Hispaniolan forms, *H. vasta* most closely approaches the large body size of the Cuban treefrog, and the cause(s) for its restricted geographic range are unclear. *Hyla vasta* is known to breed in montane streams (Schwartz and Henderson 1991), which could hinder its colonization success if that breeding habit is also a requirement. *Hyla heilprini* and *H. pulchrilineata*, both diminutive in body size, have likewise failed to colonize beyond the borders of Hispaniola. On the other hand, the failure of *O. dominicensis*, superficially very similar in appearance to the Cuban treefrog, to disperse remains something of a mystery. Although apparently smaller in body size than the Cuban treefrog, *O. dominicensis* is most similar to the Cuban treefrog in morphology (Cochran 1941), habits (Schwartz and Henderson 1991), and diet (Duer et al. 1993). Overall similarity and a human-mediated hybrid zone overlapping that of the Cuban treefrog in extreme eastern Cuba leads me to consider the possibility that *O. dominicensis* could not only equal the Cuban treefrog in body size but also provide the best possible test of body size–related colonization success.

Such a test has yet to be undertaken, and some well-defined morphological differences exist between both species that could be associated with behavioral and ecological differences. Perhaps these differences in turn could explain the overwhelmingly greater dispersal by the Cuban treefrog: the tibia are longer and webbing on the front toes is more reduced in *O. dominicensis*, the iris is blue instead of gold, and the interorbital space is greater than in the Cuban treefrog. If *O. dominicensis* is truly smaller in body size than the Cuban treefrog, then a life history study of *O. dominicensis* could assess the relative importance of morphological differences as constraints on its colonization abilities.

12

Correlates of Success of a Colonizing Species

High fecundity

Data from counts, collections, and dissections provided measures of the Cuban treefrog's colonization success, and looking at populations across Florida enabled me to measure the best and worst environmental circumstances for this species. By including its native range, I could consider Florida the decoy to the West Indian "duck." In Florida, the Cuban treefrog met all of the ten correlates associated with successful colonization but one, that of the open niche, which, as I hope to demonstrate below, did not amount to even a hindrance in its dispersal and establishment in Florida. On the other hand, correlates of colonization success need not be met for a species to colonize. Rather, like the suite of correlates tested in this study, meeting correlates *increases the likelihood* of success.

Among the correlates met by the Cuban treefrog is high fecundity (Baker 1965). Measured by production of potentially very large clutches, continuous production of eggs, and an extended egg-laying season that was never less than six months in duration, the Cuban treefrog is no exception to the general rule that large frogs lay large clutches and somewhat large eggs (Salthe and Duellman 1973). The body-size component of fecundity was particularly advantageous in light of the potentially large body sizes of females; the largest female measured in the Everglades was 99 mm SVL, and the record size of a female from Florida is 165 mm SVL (Meshaka 1996f). Likewise, the continuous presence of gravid females enabled this species to easily adjust its breeding to local conditions. Nowhere in its Florida range was the actual egg-laying season shortened to less than six months in the summer and early fall. Reproductive season of Cuban treefrogs from extreme southern Florida very closely approached that of Havana, Cuba, but equaled or exceeded breeding seasons of other native populations, including those of the Bahamas and Cayman Islands. Zug and

Zug (1979) noted a phenomenon whereby many introduced populations of the marine toad (*Bufo marinus*) have longer breeding seasons than native populations. Northern populations of the Cuban treefrog in Florida were constrained more by temperature than by rainfall, whereas the opposite was true of small insular sites. Consequently, extreme southern mainland Florida represented the most productive site for the Cuban treefrog to realize its full reproductive potential among introduced Florida sites and among many populations in its native geographic range.

Production of large clutches conferred an advantage on this species. Because large females contributed most to reproduction, greater opportunity was afforded to colonization (or recolonization) after a given breeding event. In that regard, large clutch size was one of two reasons for the phenomenal recruitment (16%) following the drought preceding this study. As the Cuban treefrog continues to colonize Florida and the West Indies, large clutches will be especially advantageous where breeding opportunities are limited, such as in northern sites with shorter breeding season and in insular sites having limited breeding habitat. The extended egg-laying season of this species across its range provides it with multiple opportunities each year to produce large clutches of large eggs, thereby minimizing interclutch time following reproductive failure or a recent colonization event. In this connection, extreme weather conditions, conventionally associated with dispersal, provided the mostly small females of a population with a reproductive advantage over larger females.

Extended breeding also produced staggered generations. The presence of individuals of all sizes and ages in nearly every month provided the population with a buffer from and ability to respond to the effects of a negative disturbance that would devastate a species limited by seasonal reproduction (Inger and Greenburg 1966). Extended breeding season with multiple opportunities to reproduce was the second reason for quick recovery in 1989–1990 following a drought. Various size-classes present in the population were either contributing to reproduction or were themselves recruited into the breeding population, quickly erasing what for other species could be ruinous long-term effects of a drought. Rapid recruitment from staggered generations will be most useful to the Cuban treefrog at the edges of its expanding Florida range where density-independent catastrophes, such as freezes, occur more frequently than in the southern Everglades. This same advantage is probably conferred more frequently on drought-prone insular sites like small cays in the West Indies and tree islands in the Everglades.

The combination of high fecundity and a long breeding season in other amphibians and reptiles has boded well in dispersal and recovery from negative disturbances. For example, large clutches and opportunistic breeding have been an advantage to the marine toad (*Bufo marinus*) in Australia, where its rapid geographic expansion across the country was well documented (for example, Lewis 1989). Closer to home, multiple clutch production and an extended breeding season by the marine toad (Meshaka et al. 2001) and the brown anole, *Anolis sagrei* (Lee et al. 1989; Meshaka et al. 2001) have also buffered the effects of periodic frosts and dry years in southern Florida.

Large clutches and mixed generations as a by-product of a long breeding season not only protect the Cuban treefrog from the effects of a negative disturbance but also enabled the Cuban treefrog to exploit a positive disturbance. Hurricane Andrew provided such an opportunity for the Cuban treefrog (Meshaka 1993); however, in this case it was primarily a segment of the population—small females, released from competition with otherwise more fecund large counterparts that overwhelmingly and uncharacteristically contributed most to the reproductive effort of that event. Because of the body-size component of its reproductive response to Hurricane Andrew, small females could be especially good colonizers. Dispersed in a storm, they have strong potential given their well-developed vagility (Meshaka 1996a) and affinity for refuges in the form of cavities and folds (Meshaka 1996b), in conjunction with a high frequency of hurricanes in the Caribbean basin (Chen and Gerber 1990).

Responses to Hurricane Andrew effectively demonstrated how some species not only adapt to strong natural disturbances, but even exploit them. Energetic constraints alone shaped the dynamics of the hurricane response. The relevance of this simple physiological mechanism of colonization success was fascinating because it revealed not only that hurricanes provide all Cuban treefrogs the chance to colonize, but that small, young females may well be the segment of the population that founds populations if individuals are dispersed into folds of vegetation during storms, as they are when dispersed in trees by people (Meshaka 1996b).

The effectiveness of dispersal and colonization by small females can be measured even at a small scale. The Cuban treefrog was most often found in mesic forest, but it does not like deep forest. If, for instance, a hurricane opens up a nearby forest more to the liking of this species, females already in the forest, and those carried into it even from a kilometer or two away can, in short order, overwhelm the newly disturbed site with eggs and tadpoles in the depressions from fallen trees. The Cuban treefrog is not alone in this positive response; other species, such as the marine toad and the greenhouse frog (*Eleutherodactylus planirostris planirostris*), are also adapted to hurricanes (Meshaka 1993).

Large clutches and continuous clutch production are, lastly, advantageous in the face of a predator-rich system. Although metamorphoslings were evident in distinct seasonal pulses when predators were numerous, they also appeared as a slow trickle during the rest of the year. During the dry season, many seasonally active snake predators are not nearly so active in the park (Dalrymple et al. 1991), thereby alleviating a potential bottleneck to recruitment. Thus, high fecundity was a benefit to introduced populations of the Cuban treefrog because it was associated with breeding seasons that rivaled in length those of native populations, decreased the wait for breeding, buffered negative disturbances and predation, and enabled it to exploit positive disturbances.

Short generation times

The next step after emergence from the egg is development. Ehrlich (1989) noted short generation times in many successful colonizing species, and the Cuban treefrog can be added to the list of species that meet this criterion. Short generation times were evidenced by a short larval period, early attainment of sexual maturity, and a generally short adult life span.

Development in hot water, incidental cannibalism (Crump 1986; Babbitt and Meshaka 2000), and probable interspecific predation best explained rapid transformation of tadpoles. On seasonally dry and often xeric small islands of the West Indies, where duration of standing water defines the term ephemeral in the extreme, ability to transform early, in conjunction with rain-stimulated breeding, offers the best combination of reproductive characteristics for survival. In the southern Everglades, subject to distinct wet-dry seasons, rapid transformation was critical to its success in part because of risk of an early drawdown of sites after dry season rainfall, but also for the very opposite reason. Early rainfall in late May–early June provided what I believe to have been optimal circumstances for reproductive success in this species. Puddles were deep enough and plentiful enough to accommodate the intense breeding responses, and many puddles also remained until rainfalls, exceeding 7 cm, deepened and connected them with fish-inhabited refugia. At this point, the threat to survival was not evaporation but predation by fish. Progression of the season increased the conflict between reproductive stimulation and an ever-diminishing body of pools without fish. For this very reason I predict that, with long-term changes in hydrology that favor longer hydroperiods and deeper water, the Cuban treefrog in the park will recede from the small tree islands it currently inhabits.

Rapid transformation and early maturity accelerated the rate of recruitment into the population. Relevant to colonization success was a decrease in the time for a population to re-equilibrate following reproductive failure (Licht 1975). Two consecutive drought years preceded this study. The Cuban treefrog rebounded with high recruitment because of fecundity, especially by older and larger females and because of multiple opportunities to breed over an extended breeding season, and the breeding population re-equilibrated quickly. As an ephemeral site breeder pre-adapted to temporal and spatial unpredictability of larval development sites, the Cuban treefrog took advantage of the numerous breeding sites available throughout the wet season and some of the solution holes available during the dry season. As revealed in the scattergram of juvenile snout-vent lengths (fig. 6.1), an enormous number responded quickly to the suitable larval conditions immediately after the drought. Short generation times in concert with high fecundity will be responsible for what will seem like an unbelievable ability to persist even in peripheral populations so often plagued by density-independent catastrophes (Mayr 1963).

Tolerance of a wide range of physical conditions

Both life history stages of the Cuban treefrog tolerate a wide range of physical conditions, thereby meeting Mayr's (1965) correlate of successful colonization. The primary obstacle to larval survival was the presence of predaceous fish. Yet, even under such circumstances, tadpoles could be found in the very shallow and grassy edges of otherwise unsuitable larval habitat. Cuban treefrog tadpoles were otherwise very hardy. Larval water temperatures of 12–41 °C enabled tadpoles to either develop in approximately three weeks or overwinter for five to six months.

In the southern Everglades predaceous fish were the greatest threat or limitation to survival of Cuban treefrog tadpoles, whereas water-starved insular sites tested the ability of this species to develop rapidly. Because standing water on small cays also is often shallow, and the water temperatures of temporary freshwater pools often exceed 42 °C (Young and Zimmerman 1956; Brown 1969), small insular sites provide the most frequent test of this species' tolerance of high water temperatures.

Although untested in the Cuban treefrog, the ability to develop in high water temperatures ($\geq$ 41.0 °C) could benefit eggs, tadpoles, and potentially the breeding adults if excessive heat limits the aquatic predators of its eggs, tadpoles, and breeding adults as it does other species in other systems (Grubb 1972; Heyer et al. 1975).

The Achilles' heel, as it were, of postmetamorphic individuals was water. They remained hidden when it was dry and are physiologically poorly adapted to water retention (Meshaka 1996b). Consequently, mesic conditions provided the best habitat in the many types of sites noted in this study. The two-fold advantage of this correlate was that requirements for both life history stages were easily met and the adults in most cases did not venture far to find breeding sites. If their physical needs are viewed simply as vertical structure with refuges in somewhat mesic conditions for adults and pools that hold water with no fish for about one month for tadpoles, it makes perfect sense that this species was at home equally around houses with swimming pools or birdbaths as in banana groves with interfurrow depressions and hammocks with solution holes and depressions in the leaf litter. Another fair assessment is that, however harsh the dry seasons are in the southern Everglades, many other sites in its native geographic range, like small Caribbean cays, are routinely harsher during the dry season.

Although the Cuban treefrog was most active in warm ambient temperatures, it emerged on very cool, if humid, nights. The lower limits of the thermal tolerance (6.4–39.0 °C) of postmetamorphic Cuban treefrogs reported by John-Alder et al. (1988) were not exceeded around buildings in the present study. This being the case in the southern Everglades, the Cuban treefrog will continue to colonize northward, relying ever more on the warmth of buildings as it proceeds northward and away from coasts, where freezing average monthly lows will ultimately define its border. Because of the thermal benefits of buildings, two geographic ranges exist for the Cuban treefrog, natural (exclusive of buildings) and total (non-building and building habitats). In the mainland United States, thermally acceptable sites with acceptable monthly levels of rainfall (Wood 1996) predict a natural geographic range throughout not only Florida, but southern coastal Georgia to the east and westward along coastal Alabama, Mississippi, Louisiana, and Texas. The instability of its northern interior Florida range will be offset by the increased availability of buildings. Given the vagaries of human-mediated habitats, an accurate prediction of its total mainland geographic range cannot be made; however, the clear-cut life history requirements of the species make all but impossible a continuous geographic range that extends farther north than extreme southern and coastal edges of the aforementioned coastal plain states.

Two other Cuban forms in Florida, the brown anole and the greenhouse frog, are also old, nonindigenous residents of Florida and successful by the measures of habitat and geographic range (Meshaka et al. 2001). In Cuba, these species, like the Cuban treefrog, are found throughout the country and in a wide range of physical conditions. Both species also continue to colonize northern sites in part because of their broad ecological tolerance and in part because of human-mediated changes in the environment that cushion them from environmental conditions that would otherwise be intolerable. In sharp contrast, the knight anole (*Anolis equestris equestris*), which has been in southern Florida for the past fifty years (Meshaka et al. 2001), is very sensitive to frost and less able to avoid its lethal effects. Consequently, its extreme southern Florida and coastal southern Florida range is unlikely to expand.

Similarity of habitats in native and introduced ranges

Similarity of habitats between native and introduced ranges is an ecological correlate of successful colonization (Brown 1989). This correlate was evident particularly in Cuban treefrog populations of the southern Everglades and the Florida Keys, where many of the habitats it invaded are present in the West Indies. Especially prevalent was its favorite natural habitat, tropical hardwood hammocks, whose floral composition in Florida is nearly entirely West Indian in derivation (Robertson 1955). Essentially, the Cuban treefrog in southern Florida had changed only its location; consequently no adjustments in its ecology have been needed to invade mesophytic forests. The same was true of mangrove forests that also occur in the West Indies. The advantage of this correlate has been minimal if any selective pressures associated with niche invasion, which ensures its phenomenal success in southern Florida more so than in northern sites. Not only were adjustments not needed to colonize its identical principal habitat in southern Florida as in Cuba, but by arriving preadapted to it, the Cuban treefrog should be expected to outcompete its north temperate competitors, more at home in wetland systems. An ecological analogue to the tropical hardwood hammock, found as islands in marsh or imbedded in pineland, are cabbage palm–oak hammocks that extend farther north in Florida. Judging from populations that I have examined around the north shore of Lake Okeechobee, the Cuban treefrog did equally well in that habitat and faced no new native ecological counterparts with which it would compete.

Disturbed habitats of southern Florida within which the Cuban treefrog thrived were also prevalent in the West Indies. As the interface between disturbed habitat and natural habitat increases, so will populations and population sizes of Cuban treefrogs. This is likely to be most notable in areas like long hydroperiod wetland that would otherwise not have supported this species.

Its affinity for both scarified sites and hammocks caused me to wonder if disturbed habitats such as banana and Brazilian pepper groves, in which this species was so successful, were structural mimics of natural subclimax forest. If this is true, observations that this species avoids deep forests (Barbour and Ramsden 1919) could reflect a historical preference for subclimax forest. This ecological sere is patchy but common in hammocks of the West Indies and Florida and historically subjected to frequent hurricanes and occasional fires.

So much of its biology makes the most sense if interpreted in this framework. Its abundances are highest in natural and human-mediated analogues of subclimax forest. Hurricanes initiate fierce breeding responses whereby the Cuban treefrog exploits newly formed larval sites that are shallow and exposed to light for optimal development.

In the artificial world of humanity, new housing developments are mimics of a natural disturbance, complete with dispersing animals in trees and provision of newly open habitat. It should be no wonder, then, that the tropical hardwood hammocks of southern Florida, frequently disturbed by humans, and perennially disturbed urban developments reflect healthy populations of Cuban treefrogs.

Coexistence with humans

Many advantages are associated with an ability to coexist, let alone thrive with humans (Brown 1989). First, as just mentioned, human-mediated disturbance of forested habitat mimics natural processes to the benefit of the Cuban treefrog. This process also continues at breakneck speed in Florida with seemingly no end (Browning 1997). Taken further, practically everything associated with destruction of any habitat and replacement with buildings has assisted species like the Cuban treefrog and, for that matter, the greenhouse frog and the hemidactyline geckos of Florida. First and foremost, this extreme process eliminates from the area entire communities of species, including potential competitors and predators. Other species are simply marginalized and so present little resistance to these exotics. The result is that the habitat resistance (Elton 1958) is shattered, thereby providing a safe home for species that do well in disturbed, biologically depauperate systems. This can happen with or without buildings.

The trappings of humanity varied, and the Cuban treefrog tolerated or thrived in the majority of them. Tree lines along agricultural fields and overgrown agricultural fields themselves were acceptable habitat. Groves, ranging from banana orchards to avocado orchards, mimicked natural subclimax forest to which this species is best suited. Yet, nothing signifies the presence of humanity more so than buildings, and many exotic species thrive in this habitat. For some species, buildings are their sole habitat in introduced sites. Building endemicity, as it were, is quite understandable when the ecology in native areas is understood. The Mediterranean gecko (*Hemidactylus turcicus*), an exclusive building-dweller in the United States, is a rock-dweller in the Old World. Skyscrapers and city parks in the United States are very close structural analogues to cliff faces and open fields for the rock dove (*Columba livia*) in the Old World. It is precisely because the Cuban treefrog is a forest-dweller that its success on buildings is so noteworthy. For the Cuban treefrog, the best combination was disturbance with lighted buildings simply because disturbed habitat marginalized other vertebrate species while retaining habitat amenable to an invertebrate prey base. At the same time, the building provided refuges capable of accommodating more Cuban treefrogs than possible in the wild, with food concentrated at lights at abundances much higher than in the wild, and this resulted in Cuban treefrog abundances up to two orders of magnitude higher than in some natural systems in the park. Specific to buildings, water was abundant even during the driest times of the year; suitable breeding sites abounded in sewers, cisterns, birdbaths, flat-topped roofs, drain pipes, and other human-related artifacts. Indeed, access to an abundance of cisterns is considered key to its colonization success on Anguilla (Townsend et al. 2000).

Whereas water is important for the colonization of small cays in the West Indies, insulation from temperature extremes, like that provided by buildings, becomes more relevant in northward dispersal of the Cuban treefrog in Florida in areas that are otherwise marginal at best for its colonization, because of either poor habitat or climate. For this very reason, two exotic southeast Asian geckos, also forest-dwellers in their native ranges, are not restricted to extreme southern Florida. The tokay gecko (*Gekko gecko*) is established in Gainesville and Tallahassee and the Indo-Pacific gecko (*Hemidactylus garnotii*) occurs north of Florida (Meshaka et al. 2001). Furthermore, the sheer numbers associated with buildings could also provide a source for recolonization of surrounding habitat following drought or frost, against which the building-dwelling populations were cushioned. These very same buildings could then just as easily serve as a springboard for other dispersal events farther north. The probability of this occurring is especially high in light of the high vagility of this species, particularly in the agency of humans (Meshaka 1996a).

One could safely say, then, that a species that coexists with humans is likely to be very successful. The trappings of humanity served the Cuban treefrog well and, from that standpoint, the Cuban treefrog was successful in large part because it exploited a fractured and redesigned system. This is quite clear biologically. The very focus of colonization success associated with human development is not so much what a species does or can do in the presence of humans as what circumstances amenable for dispersal and establishment have been created by humanity. For that reason, exotic species like the Cuban treefrog are really nothing more or less than winners of an inadvertent crapshoot to see what will get along with humans. The advantages are especially striking for species unable to invade intact systems, as in the case of most of Florida's exotic avifauna, and whose success is largely connected to human-mediated changes in flora (Carleton 1971; Owre 1973). In effect, what were once intact systems, young or old, have now become giant terraria created to our liking. Man is an unwitting accomplice who has indifferently readied Florida for the establishment of the next lucky species.

Broad diet

The Cuban treefrog clearly met the ecological correlate of broad diet, conventionally associated with colonization success (Ehrlich 1989). In this study, the Cuban treefrog ate a lot of beetles and roaches but also a wide range of prey categories, taxa, and sizes. Its diet subsumed that of and included its potential competitors. Two advantages are conferred by broad diet. First, the Cuban treefrog's weak dietary constraints minimized a major form of resistance to its colonization process in Florida generally and in particular habitats. For example, the Cuban treefrog exploited the very few categories of prey in mangroves, the dominant coastal habitat of southern Florida and one that it occupies in Cuba (Luis Moreno, pers. comm.). Tropical hardwood hammocks, structurally the most suitable natural habitat for this species, also provided this species with an adequate prey base. On the other end of the spectrum, buildings provided the Cuban treefrog with an abundance of prey, some of them uncommonly encountered in the wild, which it was capable of exploiting. As this species expands its geographic range, and possibly its habitat, broad diet will minimize the likelihood that its colonization will be obstructed by inedible prey, thereby enabling it to exploit even a species-poor prey base.

A second advantage to a broad diet is that it enables a species to adjust its diet to a superior competitor thereby minimizing the negative effects of interspecific competition. This advantage did not apply to the southern Florida Cuban treefrogs but could be relevant in areas of sympatry with the barking treefrog (*Hyla gratiosa*) and in the future with the gray treefrog (*H. chrysoscelis*) in northern Florida.

Open niche space

If physical conditions are tolerable for a species' existence, colonization success can be predicted with respect to the kinds of interspecific interactions the exotic species encounters. In this case, open niche space (Brown 1989) provides the measure. Habitat, diet, and activity were three niche axes that I evaluated for this prediction. For all three parameters, open niche space was the only correlate of colonization success not met by the Cuban treefrog in Florida. What was evident, however, was that habitat and diet of the Cuban treefrog were greatly underexploited resources. For both parameters, niche overlap was greater among Cuban treefrogs and among its four competitors than between the Cuban treefrog and its competitors. For example, the Cuban treefrog, a terrestrial-arboreal predator, generally preferred mesic forest, disturbed or natural, and did well on buildings. Both geckos were nearly exclusive building-dwellers or occurred in extremely low numbers in natural habitats. Both native hylid treefrogs were semi-aquatic species, weakly entering upland forest, with or without the Cuban treefrog. Consequently, even without open niche space, the Cuban treefrog encountered little resistance in its invasions of mostly upland habitats. One should note, however, that habitat overlap among these species would only have been meaningful if they also shared some other potentially limited resource, such as food.

Yet, diet also was a surprisingly underexploited resource. Across its geographic range, the Cuban treefrog ate a lot of roaches, beetles, and amphipods, but included a wide range of other taxa, including its potential competitors (e.g., Meshaka 1996g). On buildings and in natural habitats of the Everglades, the Cuban treefrog ate the same invertebrates as its competitors as well as those not preyed on by its competitors, and it also ate what comes closest to being its competitors. It succeeded by eating larger-bodied prey and larger-bodied taxa of prey than its competitors.

For that reason, dietary overlap, in terms of prey taxa, among the five species was far greater among the competitors than between any of the competitors and the Cuban treefrog, and potential for competition with its four syntopes was moderate at best. Consequently, the Cuban treefrog had the advantage of not having to compete with one or a suite of fierce competitors. Indeed, the highest level of dietary overlap was intraspecific. The same appears to be true in Cuba where this species occurs in the company of no other hylids (Barbour and Ramsden 1919; Schwartz and Henderson 1991), and might have only itself with which to compete as a terrestrial-arboreal predator, at least off the ground. Thus, in both natural and disturbed habitats across its geographic range, the Cuban treefrog has had little to compete with other than itself.

Two other terrestrial-arboreal hylids are present in Florida. The barking treefrog overlaps the Cuban treefrog in southern and central Florida. However, its strong preference for pinelands greatly minimizes the degree of syntopy that the two species will experience, at least in natural systems. In much the same fashion, the green treefrog and squirrel treefrog are safe from the Cuban treefrogs in their preferred habitats. The gray treefrog, on the other hand, is a forest-dweller like the Cuban treefrog and, among potential native competitors, is the likeliest candidate to meet the Cuban treefrog head-on if the Cuban treefrog can invade temperate forests in northern Florida.

Superior competitive ability

Although the potential for competition for food was moderate, the Cuban treefrog was a superior competitor for that resource, another correlate of colonization success (Baker 1965). Prey of potential competitors is subsumed by the Cuban treefrog despite general differences in diet between the Cuban treefrog and its syntopes. Per unit body size, the Cuban treefrog across sites outcompeted its Everglades competitors in maximum prey length at the cost of prey number. Moreover, as a second layer of superior competitive ability, potential competitors were themselves eaten by the Cuban treefrog.

Predation was responsible for the demonstrably unstable coexistence of the Cuban treefrog with its four competitors in the park, and this predation was not difficult: hylids were not scared of their predator, the Cuban treefrog greatly overlapped its competitors/prey in activity, all four species were small in body size, and interguild predation was unidirectional. To the advantage of the Cuban treefrog, depredations on its competitors occurred during the breeding season, when its fat stores were depleted, and at the end of the breeding season, when primarily female Cuban treefrogs were storing fat for the long dry season. Also, preying on vertebrates removed native hylids and both exotic geckos, with which juvenile Cuban treefrogs shared the greatest dietary overlap, and provided a competition-free environment. The negative effect of the Cuban treefrog's presence on the abundances of its competitors was cumulative. The more numerous it became, the more difficult it was for the other four species to coexist. For the native hylids, the negative impacts they experienced were especially severe in disturbed areas where they were already marginalized. Thus, the Cuban treefrog was not only not hindered by the presence of four potential competitors, but benefited by their presence as food during critical times of the year and, secondarily, by provision of a competitor-free environment.

The only significant overlap that occurred between the Cuban treefrog and its competitors was in the physical conditions associated with activity. High overlap of this resource, including the Cuban treefrog's limited range in relative humidity, was irrelevant as an obstacle to colonization. Quite the opposite, because of the important role its competitors played in the diet of the Cuban treefrog, overlapping activity increased the chances of encountering its competitors/prey.

Invasion of open or nearly open niches and superior competitive ability have far and away been intensely associated with the best colonizing species. In Florida, two of the most invasive exotic plants, the Brazilian pepper (*Schinus terebinthifolius*) and the melaleuca tree (*Melaleuca quinquenervia*) overwhelm native plants in disturbed settings, where conditions are marginalized for the native species. Likewise, exotic species of amphibians and reptiles in Florida are faced with a dearth of competitors and predators in the mostly urban areas of their colonization (Meshaka et al. 2001).

Worldwide, the marine toad probably best illustrates the advantages of underexploited niches and superior competitive ability (Zug and Zug 1979; Lampo and De Leo 1998). In Florida, it is the dominant and sometimes only amphibian in open, disturbed, and hydrologically altered habitats, long since abandoned by native counterparts including the southern toad, *Bufo terrestris* (Wilson and Porras 1983; Meshaka et al. 2001). The brown tree snake (*Boiga irregularis*) competes with practically nothing in Guam. It has become so successful so quickly in natural and disturbed habitats that it has shifted its prey as its dietary mainstay has become scarce. Herpetologically, few regions better illustrate the advantages of meeting these two correlates than Hawaii, with 27 exotic species including the Cuban treefrog (McKeown 1996). The outcome of this recent and sudden mixing of exotic species in Hawaii and Florida can scarcely be predicted until invasions cease (assuming for the sake of argument that they will) and the new residents can sort out their existences.

What is remarkable about exploitation of a previously poorly occupied niche and superior competitive ability in the Cuban treefrog is that both occurred in disturbed *and* natural systems. In Florida, the Cuban treefrog has not been the equivalent of the brown tree snake by any means, if only because natural habitat overlap was weak with the native competitors that it outcompeted and ate. This scenario contrasts with such exotic species nightmares as the marine toad in Australia (Covacevich and Archer 1970), the brown tree snake in Guam (Savidge 1987), and the Nile perch (*Lates niloticus*) in African rift lakes (Miller 1989). All do well in the same habitats that once were full of now extinct or nearly extinct forms. Doubtless, the Cuban treefrog's negative impact on native hylids could be severe, but native Florida amphibians have "dodged the bullet," as it were. I do not believe this will be the case in Puerto Rico, where the Cuban treefrog continues to expand its geographic range. Unless profound efforts are made to eradicate it from what appear to be isolated sites in natural forests near human habitation, the Cuban treefrog will in all likelihood disperse quickly throughout the forest. With a suite of potential competitors and predators, the Cuban treefrog probably will not drive any anurans to extinction in Puerto Rico, but probably will, in a profound way, negatively impact the abundances of forest anurans unaccustomed to an arboreal predator.

Superior competitive ability was also evident in its reproductive characteristics. The longer breeding season, larger clutches, and shorter larval time than either the green or squirrel treefrog provided the Cuban treefrog with more opportunities to quickly saturate a site. Its use of ephemeral pools of very short hydroperiod also provided it with greater numbers of larval sites than either of its competitors in uplands. Owing to the differences in larval periods and spawning sites, Cuban treefrogs were rarely found with green treefrogs, and occasionally with the squirrel treefrog. If the Cuban treefrog can tolerate higher water temperatures during development than its competitors and if this constitutes a competitive edge, then the lethal effects associated with high temperatures could provide larval Cuban treefrogs competitor-free space and an additional food source of dead or dying competitors, including tadpoles of the Florida chorus frog (*Pseudacris nigrita verrucosa*) and the eastern narrowmouth toad (*Gastrophryne carolinensis*) with which it was more frequently found in the park.

Few predators

Some of the ecological correlates of successful colonization could very easily be ascribed to uniquely human endeavors like business. For instance, a business, like a colonizing species, stands a good chance of succeeding if no one else does what it does (open niche) or, if a similar service exists it doesn't do it as well (superior competitive ability). Broad diet is part and parcel of the ecological versatility that Mayr (1965) noted as an overall good indicator for a colonizing species. Analogously, a jack-of-all-trades could adapt his business in the face of superior competitors, fickle economy, or even a community that is ambivalent or hostile to its presence. For nonbiologists interested in the Cuban treefrog mystery, enemy-free state (Pimm 1989) has to be the most understandably obvious of what are otherwise commonsense predictors of colonization success. Doubtlessly, an absence of enemies is a logical expectation for a successful species in a strange land. For example, human-mediated predator removal increases elk herds (Chase 1987). Likewise, in Florida, bobcats and panthers are inconsequential and even absent in some places to control feral hogs.

Because of its large body size and chemical protection, the Cuban treefrog at first glance seems to be the arboreal equivalent of the marine toad: too large, messy, and toxic to be eaten. Two red herrings are at play here. The first is the species, the second is in the prediction. The Cuban treefrog is anything but predator-free, even if mammals are excluded from the list of potential predators. In Florida and in the West Indies, it is subject to the depredations of a wide range of snakes and birds. At least one lizard eats it, too. This is hardly a predator-free species in the manner of the mongoose or goat. The second red herring is that if an enemy-free state is good, then a predator-rich state must be awful. Pimm (1991) clearly demonstrates that this is not the case and that predators can hinder or enhance colonization for a variety of reasons. For example, the Cuban treefrog might be held at bay by an abundant species that specializes on arboreal frogs. However, the overall predator pressure in the predator-rich system of the park is dampened for several reasons: (1) predators ate one another, which presumably reduced their own numbers, (2) none of its predators specialized on treefrogs, (3) few of its predators could eat all sizes of the Cuban treefrog, and (4) few of its predators were found in all habitats occupied by the Cuban treefrog. As for the Cuban treefrog, it was not very easy to catch, highly fecund, and quick to outgrow some of those predators.

Thus, in natural systems of Florida and in Cuba, the Cuban treefrog persevered despite a barrage of ophidian and avian predators of postmetamorphic individuals. In light of the uniformity of Cuban treefrog predators throughout Florida, no reason exists to predict resistance in natural systems elsewhere in its expanding Florida range.

In not so natural areas of its Florida range, the Cuban treefrog came very close to meeting Pimm's (1989) ecological correlate by being practically predator-free. Much of this species' Florida range, like much of present-day Florida, comprised disturbed habitat that ranges in extremes from remnant forest to agricultural fields and cities. Even in the more benignly disturbed areas, disturbed habitats in urban settings often have few if any native amphibians and reptiles but become rich in exotic species (Meshaka 1999a,b), very few of which pose any predatory threat. In these ecologically fractured communities the Cuban treefrog is nearly always one of only three amphibians (marine toad and greenhouse frog) present, its abundance on buildings in part explained by number of resident predator species, which negatively affect its numbers.

Larger body size than nearest relatives

The large body size of this species conforms to Ehrlich's (1989) prediction for a successful colonizer of a body size larger than its nearest relatives. The historic and present day geographic ranges of the Cuban treefrog greatly exceed those of all other West Indian hylids, none of which have colonized the United States. In the southern Everglades, potential hylid competitors underexploited the mesic upland forests preferred by the Cuban treefrog and were depredated almost to extirpation on buildings. In northern Florida, it will also encounter no other hylids near its own body size (Conant and Collins 1991).

Throughout this work, I have alluded to the advantages of large body size in colonization success. As just mentioned, adult Cuban treefrogs were relatively free of some predators simply because they were too large to eat, and the largest individuals were quite safe from some of the worst predators. Because the Cuban treefrog will encounter no new predators elsewhere in Florida, it will not lose this colonizing advantage as it disperses northward in the state. This is a safe prediction as long as no new predators are added to Florida. The same prediction and caveat apply to Hawaii and the Caribbean, exclusive of Puerto Rico. I simply do not know why this species did not colonize Puerto Rico until it was inadvertently dispersed there in the 1960s. However, the direction of two dispersal media, plant commerce and hurricanes, is westerly from Puerto Rico and could account for animals and plants leaving the island rather than dispersing to the island.

Another advantage to large body size was fecundity. Ultimately, the large body sizes and the food eaten by female Cuban treefrogs produced the receptacle of energy for the production of very large clutches of large eggs. As mentioned earlier, this advantage will become more valuable as this species ventures into less hospitable conditions in the same two ways possible elsewhere. First, colonies could be established quickly if even one gravid female and a male were given the opportunity to be transported. Second, a female could compensate for poor or nonexistent recruitment for a few years by spending that time growing in the absence of many/any conspecifics. Then, when recruitment is finally possible, the one or a few females potentially could flood the site with many thousands of young. Circumstantial evidence supports this contention. The very largest individuals, such as a 122-mm SVL female from Lake Placid (this study), an 85-mm SVL male from Lake Placid (Meshaka 1996f), a 165-mm SVL female from Sebring (Meshaka 1996f), and a 160-mm SVL female from Gainesville, were all from sites where either no other or only a few much smaller conspecifics were also seen. For this reason, the negative association between female body size and colony size has led me to interpret the presence of single, or nearly single, giant Cuban treefrogs as founders awaiting or just realizing the establishment of a colony. There, they exist well below the carrying capacity of the site, all the while eating underexploited prey and the potential competitors of future conspecifics.

Lastly, its large body size nullified the danger of morphological similarity, a proven barrier to coexistence (Lack 1947), particularly by invaders (Pimm 1991). Admittedly, the Cuban treefrog differed from its potential competitors in habitat preference and ecological position; however, the great disparity in body size between the Cuban treefrog and its nearest relatives further minimized the potential for competition for food and enabled it to exploit prey, like roaches, that were rare if even present in the diets of its nearest ecological analogues in the southern Everglades. Being the largest species provided the largest individuals with the largest and the most prey, prey that included its potential competitors.

Among the native hylids of the southeastern United States, the gray treefrog is morphologically and ecologically most similar to the Cuban treefrog. It remains to be seen what will become of both species if they make contact in the eastern deciduous forests of northern Florida, which for both species will be the edges of their geographic ranges. Elsewhere, the Cuban treefrog is found with either no morphologically/ecologically similar species or possibly several of them. The Cuban treefrog faces no known ecological analogues in Hawaii, Puerto Rico, or on the many cays scattered across the Caribbean. On the other hand, in Jamaica and on Hispaniola, two terrestrial-arboreal treefrogs, only somewhat smaller than the Cuban treefrog, occur. The diet of one of them, *Osteopilus dominicensis* (Duer et al. 1993), comes closest to that of the Cuban treefrog; however, until a food web is completed, the full extent of dietary overlap of the other three species remains a speculation.

13

Opportunities for Colonization by the Cuban Treefrog

The Cuban treefrog has not finished its geographic expansion in the United States or in the Caribbean. As one proceeds northward from the southern Everglades, climate is the only variable that changes until it finally defines the Cuban treefrog's continuous mainland range to the southeastern coastal plain. In its northward dispersal, the Cuban treefrog will follow humanity in all but the most developed cities, perhaps getting bruised by the gray treefrog in cold temperate forests. Elsewhere in the United States, the absence of predators, an open niche space, amenable physical conditions, and plenty of disturbed habitat in Hawaii will, I believe, make the islands a paradise for the Cuban treefrog.

Human-mediated colonization of the small islands of the Lesser Antilles is inevitable, where it has begun to appear as spot fires (for example, St. Maarten and Virgin Islands), but the dynamics of those populations remain a guess given the vagaries of human activities, small island size, and naturally harsh conditions of small cays. Greatest potential for range expansion of the Cuban treefrog in the Caribbean is in Puerto Rico and Jamaica. Because of unknown predation pressure, its future in Puerto Rico remains unclear. However, with no resident analogue, its batracophagous habits, the presence of humanity, amenable physical conditions, and habitat similar to that of Cuba, I would be surprised if this species does not at least become a ubiquitous human commensal in towns and farms across the island, to the detriment of the coquí (*Eleutherodactylus coqui*). Likewise, should this species be dispersed to Jamaica, my prediction of its fate is similar to that in Puerto Rico: threatening in natural systems, but successful in the fractured communities inhabited by humans. However, despite the presence of hylid treefrogs in Jamaica, its forests could be easier for the Cuban treefrog to invade than those of Puerto Rico because this species is not restricted to bromeliads like the

Jamaican hylids. Consequently, natural or human-mediated loss of bromeliads in Jamaican forests could provide the Cuban treefrog extensive habitat already devoid of potential competitor/prey species of treefrogs. Historically, intact forests and inadequate dispersal events could have easily explained the absence of the Cuban treefrog in Jamaica. Unfortunately, this is no longer the case. The Jamaican landscape is more scarified and populated by humans than in the past, and the opening up of Cuba is inevitable, even imminent, which will give the Cuban treefrog its chance to colonize. In my opinion, only Hispaniola provides any real resistance to colonization by the Cuban treefrog. The resident congener is morphologically and ecologically very similar to the Cuban treefrog and has hybridized with the Cuban treefrog in Guantanamo, Cuba. In all probability, the Cuban treefrog will in kind be absorbed by *O. dominicensis* if introduced to Hispaniola.

I am least certain of this species' future in Central and South America. Clearly, deciduous forest, an infrequently hostile coastal climate, urban development, and human-mediated dispersal increase the likelihood of geographic expansion southward along the Texas coast. Should this happen, the Cuban treefrog will come full circle in every sense of the word, in a most ironic twist whereby it will be poised to reinvade the Yucatan and South America, its center of origin.

In sum, the Cuban treefrog has succeeded as a colonizing species and will continue to do so astonishingly because, although the reasons for its colonization success are its own, the reasons for its phenomenal success rest with us.

14

Future of the Cuban Treefrog in the Southern Everglades and Everglades National Park

For reasons presented in earlier chapters, the Cuban treefrog is unlikely to disappear from Florida. Unless an as yet unknown pathogen emerges, the Cuban treefrog cannot be eradicated from Florida for the very reasons it has colonized and continues to disperse northward in the state. It is highly vagile, especially in the agency of humans, and has dispersed to natural and unnatural systems, most of which are familiar to it and to its liking. Once there, it withstands negative disturbances and rapidly saturates areas under favorable conditions, incidentally providing itself with a competitor-free space. The Cuban treefrog is not a midlevel predator without predators, and so is unlikely to deplete its own food base and cause its own demise. Rather, the Cuban treefrog has become just another anuran in the intact southern Everglades. It is a superior competitor in two greatly underexploited niches, where its negative impacts on native hylids, although profound, are at least restricted by habitat. Even in all but the most sterile cities that are too developed and antiseptic for its existence, the Cuban treefrog is a ubiquitous member of the new and as yet unsettled exotic and almost endemic community of the increasingly urban landscape of Florida, itself a barometer of humanity.

For the same reasons, I expect the Cuban treefrog to persist in the southern Everglades and in the park. Total immersion in water or desertification of the park would be necessary to extirpate this species. Although both extremes are unlikely to occur, the former scenario was partially played out in the park during the high water years of 1995–1996. Census data of that time reflected the sensitivity of the Cuban treefrog to flowing fishy water that connected previously fishless puddles across parts of the landscape. The result was a decrease in acceptable habitat for both life history stages of the Cuban treefrog, restricting its presence to the dryer hammocks.

The water-rich scenario of the mid 1990s offers a peek into the future of the Everglades. Proposed hydrological restoration of the park will increase the water depth and hydroperiod of the Everglades in the hopes of rectifying the water delivery system, long compromised by development needs in surrounding areas. With this implementation will come higher water levels for a longer period of time in the park. Previously "puddly" areas will become inundated with water, and the water, ever so slowly, will flow and for a longer time in the year than during this study. Suitable upland sites for the Cuban treefrog will become fewer in number and smaller in size, and both the number and duration of breeding sites for the Cuban treefrog will also decrease. As long as the dry season water table is not allowed to remain precipitously low, the wet season water levels are not so unnaturally high as to kill off tree islands, and high water levels are not reached unnaturally fast in the season, the hydrology of the southern Everglades will come far closer to the natural patterns than they were at the time of this study. Should this occur, so will most certainly end the heyday of the Cuban treefrog and redefine its distribution to the most upland of forests of the River of Grass.

Literature Cited

Allen, E. R., and W. T. Neill. 1953. The treefrog, *Hyla septentrionalis*, in Florida. *Copeia* 1953:127–128.

Allen, E. R., and R. Slatten. 1945. A herpetological collection from the vicinity of Key West, Florida. *Herpetologica* 3:25–26.

Anderson, K. 1996. A karyological perspective on the monophyly of the hylid genus *Osteopilus*. *In* R. Powell and R. W. Henderson (eds.), *Contributions to West Indian Herpetology: A Tribute to Albert Schwartz*, 157–168. SSAR Contributions to Herpetology, vol. 12. Ithaca, N.Y.

Ashton, R. E., Jr. 1976. County records of reptiles and amphibians in Florida. *Fla. State Mus. Herpetol. Newsletter* 1:1–13.

Ashton, R. E., and P. S. Ashton. 1988. *Handbook of Reptiles and Amphibians of Florida*. Part 3, *The Amphibians*. Windward Publ., Miami.

Austin, S. 1975. Exotics. *Fla. Nat.* 48:2–5.

Babbitt, K. J., and W. E. Meshaka Jr. 2000. Benefits of eating conspecifics: effects of background diet, survival, and metamorphosis in the Cuban treefrog (*Osteopilus septentrionalis*). *Copeia* 2000:469–474.

Baker, H. G. 1965. Characteristics and modes of origin of weeds. *In* H. G. Baker and C. L. Stebbins (eds.), *The Genetics of Colonizing Species*, 147–169. Academic Press, New York.

Barbour, T. 1910. Notes on the herpetology of Jamaica. *Bull. Mus. Comp. Zool.* 52:273–301.

———. 1931. Another introduced frog in North America. *Copeia* 1931:140.

———. 1937. Third list of Antillean amphibians and reptiles. *Bull. Mus. Comp. Zool.* 82:77–166.

Barbour, T., and C. T. Ramsden. 1919. The herpetology of Cuba. *Bull. Mus. Comp. Zool.* 47:71–213.

Beard, D. 1938. *Everglades National Park Project*. U.S.D.I., N.P.S., Washington, D.C.

Blair, W. F. 1958. Call difference as an isolation mechanism in Florida species of hylid frogs. *Q. J. Fla. Acad. Sci.* 21:32–48.

———. 1959. Call structure and species groups in U.S. treefrogs (*Hyla*). *Southwest. Nat.* 3:77–89.

Boulenger, G. A. 1882. *Catalogue of the Batrachia Salientia Ecaudata in the collection of the British Museum*, 2nd ed. London.

Bowler, J. K. 1977. Longevity of reptiles and amphibians in North American collections. *Herpetol. Circ.* 6:1–32.

Brach, V. 1976. Habits and food of *Anolis equestris* in Florida. *Copeia* 1976:187–189.

Brown, H. A. 1969. Heat resistance of some anuran tadpoles (Hylidae and Pelobatidae). *Copeia* 1969:138–147.

Brown, J. H. 1989. Patterns, modes, and extents of invasions by vertebrates. *In* J. A. Drake, H. A. Mooney, F. di Castri, R. H. Groves, F. J. Kruger, M. Rejmanek, and M. Williamson (eds.), *Biological Invasions: A Global Perspective,* 85–110. John Wiley and Sons, New York.

Browning, M. 1997. Swamped. *Miami Herald,* February 23, *Tropic Magazine.*

Burton, F. J. 1994. Climate and tides of the Cayman Islands. Pp. 51-60. *In* M. A. Brunt and J. E. Davies (eds.), *The Cayman Islands: Natural History and Biogeography.* Kluwer Academic Publishers. Netherlands.

Butterfield, B. P. 1996. Patterns and processes of invasions by amphibians and reptiles into the West Indies and south Florida. Ph.D. diss. Auburn University, Auburn, Ala.

Butterfield, B. P., W. E. Meshaka Jr., and C. Guyer. 1997. Non-indigenous reptiles and amphibians. *In* D. Simberloff, D. C. Schmitz, and T. C. Brown (eds.), *Strangers in Paradise,* 123–138. Island Press, Washington, D.C.

Campbell, T. 1999. Geographic distribution: *Osteopilus septentrionalis. Herpetol. Rev.* 30:50.

Carleton, A. R. 1971. Studies on a population of the red-whiskered bulbul, *Pycnonotus jocusus* (Linnaeus), in Dade County, Florida. M.S. thesis. University of Miami, Coral Gables, Fla.

Carr, A. F. 1940. A contribution to the herpetology of Florida. *Univ. Fla. Publ. Biol. Sci. Serv.* 3:1–118.

Carr, A. F., and C. J. Goin. 1955. *Reptiles, Amphibians, and Fresh-Water Fishes of Florida.* Univ. Florida Press, Gainesville.

Chase, A. 1987. *Playing God in Yellowstone.* Harcourt Brace Jovanovich, New York.

Chen, E., and J. F. Gerber. 1990. Climate. *In* R. L. Myers and J. J. Ewel (eds.), *Ecosystems of Florida,* 11–34. Univ. Central Florida Press, Orlando.

Cochran, D. M. 1941. Herpetology of Hispaniola. *U.S. Natl. Mus. Bull.* 177.

Cole, C. J. 1974. Chromosome evolution in selected treefrogs, including casque-headed species (*Pternohyla, Triprion, Hyla,* and *Smilisca*). *Am. Mus. Novit.* 2541:1–10.

Conant, R., and J. T. Collins. 1991. *Reptiles and Amphibians of Eastern/Central North America,* 3rd ed. Houghton Mifflin, Boston.

Cope, E. D. 1863. On *Trachycephalus, Scaphiopus* and other American Batrachia. *Proc. Acad. Nat. Sci. Phila.* 1863:43–54.

Courtenay, W. R., Jr. 1997. Nonindigenous fish. *In* D. Simberloff, D. C. Schmitz, and T. C. Brown (eds.), *Strangers in Paradise,* 109–122. Island Press, Washington, D.C.

Covacevich, J., and M. Archer. 1970. The distribution of the cane toads *Bufo marinus* and effects on indigenous vertebrates. *Mem. Queensl. Mus.* 17:305–320.

Coy Otero, A., and N. Lorenzo Hernandez. 1982. Lista de los helmintos parasitos de los vertebrados cubanos. *Poeyana* 235:1–57.

Coy Otero, A., L. Ventosa, and A. Quintana. 1980. Nuevo record deba. *Misc. Zool. Acad. Nematodo para Cucien. Cuba* 9:1.

Crump, M. L. 1986. Cannibalism by younger tadpoles: another hazard of metamorphosis. *Copeia* 1986:1007–1009.

Dalrymple, G. H. 1988. The herpetofauna of Long Pine Key, Everglades National Park, in relation to vegetation and hydrology. *In* R. Szaro, K. E. Severson, and D. R. Patton (eds.), *Management of Amphibians, Reptiles, and Small Mammals in North America.* 72–86. U.S.D.A. Forest Service, General Technical Report RM-166, Fort Collins, Colo.

Dalrymple, G. H., T. M. Steiner, R. J. Nodell, and F. S. Bernardino Jr. 1991. Seasonal activity of the snakes of Long Pine Key, Everglades National Park. *Copeia* 1992:294–302.

Davis, J. H., Jr. 1943. The natural features of southern Florida, especially the vegetation, and the Everglades. *Fla. Geol. Surv. Bull.* No. 25.

Di Castri, F. 1989. History of biological invasions with special emphasis on the Old World. *In* J. A. Drake, H. A. Mooney, F. di Castri, R. H. Groves, F. J. Kruger, M. Rejmanek, and M. Williamson (eds.), *Biological Invasions: A Global Perspective,* 1–30. John Wiley and Sons, New York.

Douglas, M. S. 1947. *The Everglades: River of Grass.* Rinehart, New York.

Downhower, J. F. 1976. Darwin's finches and the evolution of sexual dimorphism in body size. *Nature* 263:558–563.

Duellman, W. E., and L. N. Bell. 1955. The frogs and toads of the Everglades National Park. *Everglades Nat. Hist.* 3:102–113.

Duellman, W. E., and C. Cole. 1965. Studies of chromosomes of some anuran amphibians (Hylidae and Centrolenidae). *Syst. Zool.* 14:139–143.

Duellman, W. E., and R. I. Crombie. 1970. *Hyla septentrionalis. Catalogue of American Amphibians and Reptiles,* 92.1–92.4.

Duellman W. E., and A. Schwartz. 1958. Amphibians and reptiles of southern Florida. *Bull. Fla. State Mus.* 3:181–324.

Duer, C. K., J. M. Cisek, and R. Powell. 1993. Food habits of *Osteopilus dominicensis. Caribb. J. Sci.* 28:226–228.

Dumeril, A. M. C., and G. Bibron. 1841. *Erpetologie general, ou, Histoire naturelle complete des reptiles,* vol. 8. Roret, Paris.

Dunn, E. R. 1926. The frogs of Jamaica. *Proc. Boston Soc. Nat. Hist.* 38:111–130.

Dupach, E., Jr. 1993. *Bahamas Handbook and Businessman's Annual.* Etienne Dupach Jr. Publishing, Nassau.

Ehrlich, P. R. 1989. Attributes of invaders and the invading processes: vertebrates. *In* J. A. Drake, H. A. Mooney, F. di Castri, R. H. Groves, F. J. Kruger, M. Rejmanek, and M. Williamson (eds.), *Biological Invasions: A Global Perspective,* 315–328. John Wiley and Sons, New York.

Elton, C. S. 1958. *The Ecology of Invasions by Plants and Animals.* Methuen, London.

Ferster, B., and Z. Pruzak. 1994. Preliminary checklist of the ants (Hymenoptera: Formicidae) of Everglades National Park. *Florida Entomologist* 77:508–512.

Franz, R., C. K. Dodd Jr., and D. W. Buden. 1993. Distributional records of amphibians and reptiles from the Exuma Islands, Bahamas, including the first report of a freshwater turtle and introduced gecko. *Caribbean Journal of Science* 29(3–4):165–173.

Goin, C. J. 1947. *Studies on the Life History of* Eleutherodactylus ricordii planirostris *(Cope) in Florida with Special Reference to the Local Distribution of an Allelomorphic Color Pattern.* Univ. Florida Press, Gainesville.

Goin, C. J., and C. G. Jackson. 1965. Hemoglobin values of some amphibians and reptiles of Florida. *Herpetologica* 21:145–146.

Goin, C. J., O. B. Goin, and G. R. Zug. 1978. *Introduction to Herpetology,* 3rd ed. Freeman, San Francisco.

Goin, O. B., C. J. Goin, and K. Bachman. 1968. DNA and amphibian life history. *Copeia* 1968:532–540.

Gordon, D. R., and K. P. Thomas. 1997. Florida's invasion by nonindigenous plants: history, screening, and regulation. *In* D. Simberloff, D. C. Schmitz, and T. C. Brown (eds.), *Strangers in Paradise,* 21–37. Island Press, Washington, D.C.

Gosner, K. L. 1960. A simplified table for staging anuran embryos and larvae with notes on identification. *Herpetologica* 16:183–190.

Grant, C. 1940. The herpetology of the Cayman Islands. *Bull. Inst. Jam. Sci. Ser.* 2:1–56.

Grubb, J. C. 1972. Differential predation by *Gambusia affinis* on the eggs of seven species of anuran amphibians. *Am. Midl. Nat.* 88:102–108.

Gunderson, L. H. 1994. Vegetation of the Everglades: determinants of community composition. *In* S. M. Davis and J. C. Ogden (eds.), *Everglades: The Ecosystem and Its Restoration,* 323–340. St. Lucie Press, Delray, Fla.

Gunderson, L. H., and W. F. Loftus. 1993. The Everglades: competing land uses imperil the biotic communities of a vast wetland. *In* W. H. Martin, S. C. Boyce, and A. C. Echternact (eds.), *Biotic Communities of the Southeastern United States,* 199–255. John Wiley and Sons, New York.

Hedges, S. B. 1996. The origin of West Indian amphibians and reptiles. *In* R. Powell and R. W. Henderson (eds.), *Contributions to West Indian Herpetology: A Tribute to Albert Schwartz,* 95–128. SSAR Contributions to Herpetology, vol. 12. Ithaca, N.Y.

Hedges, S. B., C. A. Hass, and L. R. Maxson. 1992. Caribbean biogeography: molecular evidence for dispersal in West Indian terrestrial vertebrates. *Proc. Nat. Acad. Sci. U.S.A.* 89:1909–1913.

Heyer, R. W., R. W. McDiarmid, and D. L. Weigmann. 1975. Tadpoles, predation and pond habitats in the tropics. *Biotropica* 7:100–111.

Inger, R. F., and B. Greenberg. 1966. Ecological and competitive relations among three species of frog (genus *Rana*). *Ecology* 47:746–759.

James, F. C. 1997. Nonindigenous birds. *In* D. Simberloff, D. C. Schmitz, and T. C. Brown (eds.), *Strangers in Paradise,* 139–156. Island Press, Washington, D.C.

Jaume, M. L. 1966. Catálogo de los anfibios de Cuba. *Mus. "Felipe Poey" Acad. Cien. Cuba, Trab. Divulg.* 35:1–21.

Joglar, R. L., and N. Rios Lopez. 1995. *Osteopilus septentrionalis* (Cuban tree-frog, rana platanera). Distribution. *Herpetol. Rev.* 26:105–106.

Joglar, R. L., N. Rios Lopez, and M. Cardona. 1998. *Osteopilus septentrionalis* (Cuban treefrog, rana platanera). Distribution. *Herpetol. Rev.* 29:107.

John-Alder, H. B., P. J. Morin, and S. Lawler. 1988. Thermal physiology, phenology, and distribution of treefrogs. *Am. Nat.* 132:507–519.

Kaiser, H., and R. W. Henderson. 1995. The conservation status of Lesser Antillean frogs. *Herpetol. Nat. Hist.* 2(2):41–46.

King, W. 1960. New populations of West Indian reptiles and amphibians in southeastern Florida. *Q. J. Fla. Acad. Sci.* 23:71–73.

King, F. W. 1966. Competition between two south Florida lizards of the genus *Anolis*. Ph.D. diss. University of Miami, Fla.

Kluge, A. G., and M. J. Eckhardt. 1969. *Hemidactylus garnotii* Dumeril and Bibron, a triploid all-female species of geckonid lizard. *Copeia* 1969:651–664.

Koopman, K. F., and R. Ruibal. 1955. Cave fossil vertebrates from Camaguey, Cuba. *Breviora* 46:1–8.

Krakauer, T. 1968. The ecology of the neotropical toad, *Bufo marinus,* in south Florida. *Herpetologica* 24:214–221.

Krebs, C. J. 1989. *Ecological Methodology.* Harper-Collins, New York.

Krysko, K. L., and F. W. King. 1999. Geographic distribution: *Osteopilus septentrionalis. Herpetol. Rev.* 30:230–231.

Lack, D. L. 1947. *Darwin's Finches.* Cambridge University Press, London.

Lampo, M., and G. A. De Leo. 1998. Invasion ecology of the toad, *Bufo marinus,* from South America to Australia. *Ecol. Appl.* 8:386–396.

Lantz, J. P. 1952. Interesting habits of *Hyla dominicensis. Herpetologica* 8:106.

Laurenti, J. N. 1768. *Specimen medicum exhibens synopsin reptilium emandatum cum experimentis cerca venena et antidota reptilium austriacorum.* Vienna.

Layne, J. N. 1997. Nonindigenous mammals. *In* D. Simberloff, D. C. Schmitz, and T. C. Brown (eds.), *Strangers in Paradise,* 157–186. Island Press, Washington, D.C.

Layne, J. N., J. A. Stallcup, G. E. Woolfenden, M. N. McCauley, and D. J. Worley. 1977. Southwest Inventory of the Seven County Region, Included is the Central Florida Phosphate Industry Area Wide Environmental Impact Study. *PD-278456. U.S. Department of Commerce, National Technical Information Service.* 1:370–372.

Lazell, J. D., Jr. 1989. *Wildlife of the Florida Keys: A Natural History.* Island Press, Washington, D.C.

Lee, D. S. 1968. Feeding habits of the Cuban treefrog, *Hyla septentrionalis,* in south Florida. *Bull. Md. Herpetol. Soc.* 4:63–64.

————. 1969. Treefrogs of Florida. *Fla. Nat.* 43:12–14.

————. 1970. A list of the amphibians and reptiles of Florida. *Bull. Md. Herpetol. Soc.* 6:74–80.

Lee, J. C., D. Clayton, S. Eisenstein, and I. Perez. 1989. The reproductive cycle of *Anolis sagrei* in southern Florida. *Copeia* 1989:930–937.

Levins, R. 1968. *Evolution in Changing Environments: Some Theoretical Explorations.* Princeton University Press, Princeton, N.J.

Lewis, S. 1989. *Cane Toads: An Unnatural History.* Dolphin/Doubleday, New York.

Licht, L. E. 1975. Comparative life history features of the western spotted frog, *Rana pretiosa,* from low- and high-elevation populations. *Can. J. Zool.* 53:1254–1257.

Light, S. S., and J. W. Dineen. 1994. Water control in the Everglades: a historical perspective. *In* S. M. Davis and J. C. Ogden (eds.), *Everglades: The Ecosystem and Its Restoration,* 47–84. St. Lucie Press, Delray Beach, Fla.

Loftus, W. F., R. A. Johnson, and G. H. Anderson. 1992. Ecological impacts of the reduction of groundwater levels in short-hydroperiod marshes of the Everglades. *In* J. A. Stanford and J. J. Simons (eds.), *Proceedings of the First International Conference on Ground Water Ecology,* 199–208. American Water Resources Association, Bethesda, Md.

Love, B. 1995. *Osteopilus septentrionalis* (Cuban treefrog). Predation. *Herpetol. Rev.* 26:201–202.

Loveless, C. M. 1959. A study of the vegetation of the Florida Everglades. *Ecology* 40:1–9.

Lynn, W. G. 1940. The herpetology of Jamaica. I. Amphibians. *Bull. Inst. Jam. Sci. Ser.* 1:1–59.

Maxson, L. R. 1992. Tempo and pattern in anuran speciation and phylogeny: an albumin perspective. *In* K. Adler (ed.), *Herpetology: Current Research on the Biology of Amphibians and Reptiles,* 41–57. SSAR Contributions to Herpetology, vol 9. Oxford, Ohio.

Maxson, L. R., and A. C. Wilson. 1975. Albumin evolution and organismal evolution in tree frogs (Hylidae). *Syst. Zool.* 24:1–15.

Mayr, E. 1926. Die Ausbreitung des Girlitz. *J. Ornithol.* 74:571–671.

————. 1963. *Animal Species and Evolution.* Harvard University Press, Cambridge.

————. 1965. The nature of colonization in birds. *In* H. G. Baker and G. L. Stebbins (eds.), *The Genetics of Colonizing Species,* 29–43. Academic Press, New York.

McKeown, S. 1996. *A Field Guide to the Reptiles and Amphibians in the Hawaiian Islands.* Diamond Head Publ., Los Osos, Calif.

Mertens, R. 1939. Herpetologische Ergebnisse einer Reise nach der Insel Hispaniola, Westinden. Abhandl. Senckenberg. *Naturforsch. Ges.* 449:1–84.

Meshaka, W. E., Jr. 1993. Hurricane Andrew and the colonization of five invading species in southern Florida. *Fla. Sci.* 56:193–201.

————. 1994a. Ecological correlates of successful colonization in the Cuban treefrog, *Osteopilus septentrionalis* (Anura: Hylidae). Ph.D. diss. Florida International University, Miami.

————. 1994b. Reproductive cycle of the Indo-Pacific gecko, (*Hemidactylus garnotii*), in south Florida. *Fla. Sci.* 57:6–9.

————. 1995. Reproductive cycle and colonization ability of the Mediterranean gecko (*Hemidactylus turcicus*) in south-central Florida. *Fla. Sci.* 58:10–15.

————. 1996a. Vagility and the Florida distribution of the Cuban treefrog (*Osteopilus septentrionalis*). *Herpetol. Rev.* 27:37–40.

————. 1996b. Retreat use by the Cuban treefrog *Osteopilus septentrionalis*: implications for successful colonization in Florida. *J. Herpetol.* 30:443–445.

————. 1996c. Occurrence of the parasite *Skrjabinoptera scelopori* (Caballero Rodriguez, 1971) in the Cuban treefrog (*Osteopilus septentrionalis*): mainland and island comparisons. *In* R. Powell and R. W. Henderson (eds.), *Contributions to West Indian Herpetology: A Tribute to Albert Schwartz,* 271–276. SSAR Contributions to Herpetology, vol. 12. Ithaca, N.Y.

————. 1996d. Anuran Davian behavior: a Darwinian dilemma. *Fla. Sci.* 59:74–75.

————. 1996e. Cooperative foraging or theft by the barred owl? *Fla. Field Nat.* 24:15.

————. 1996f. Cuban treefrog (*Osteopilus septentrionalis*): maximum size. *Herpetol. Rev.* 27:57.

————. 1996g. Diet and the colonization of buildings by the Cuban treefrog (*Osteopilus septentrionalis*). *Caribb. J. Sci.* 32:187–190.

————. 1997. The herpetofauna of Buck Island Ranch: an altered wetland in south-central Florida. *Fla. Sci.* 60:1–7.

————. 1999a. The herpetofauna of the Kampong. *Fla. Sci.* 62:153–157.

————. 1999b. The herpetofauna of the Doc Thomas House in South Miami, Florida. *Fla. Field Nat.* 27:122–124.

————. 2000. Colonization dynamics in two exotic geckos (*Hemidactylus garnotii* and *H. mabouia*) in Everglades National Park. *J. Herpetol.* 34:163–168.

Meshaka, W. E., Jr., and B. Ferster. 1995. Two species of snakes eat the Cuban treefrog (*Osteopilus septentrionalis*). *Fla. Field Nat.* 23:97–98.

Meshaka, W. E., Jr., and K. P. Jansen. 1997. Cuban treefrog (*Osteopilus septentrionalis*). Predation. *Herpetol. Rev.* 28:147–148.

Meshaka, W. E., Jr., B. P. Butterfield, and J. B. Hauge. 1993. Reproductive notes on (*Hemidactylus mabouia*) in southern Florida. *Herpetol. Nat. Hist.* 2:109–110.

————. 2001. *The Exotic Amphibians and Reptiles of Florida.* Krieger Publishing, Melbourne, Fla.

Meshaka, W. E., Jr., R. Clouse, and L. MacMahon. 1997. Diet of the tokay gecko (*Gekko gecko*) in southern Florida. *Fla. Field Nat.* 25:105–107.

Meshaka, W. E., Jr., W. F. Loftus, and T. M. Steiner. 2000. The herpetofauna of Everglades National Park. *Fla. Sci.* 63:84–103.

Miller, D. J. 1989. Introduction and extinction of fish in the African Great Lakes. *Trends Ecol. Evol.* 4:56–59.

Mittleman, M. B. 1950a. Status of the name *Hyla septentrionalis*. *Herpetologica* 6:24–26.

———. 1950b. Miscellaneous notes of some amphibians and reptiles from the southeastern states. *Herpetologica* 6:20–24.

Moler, P. E. 1990. *Checklist of Florida's Amphibians and Reptiles*. Bureau Wildlife Research, Florida Game and Fresh Water Fish Commission, Tallahassee.

Moler, P. E., and J. Kezer. 1993. Karyology and systematics of the salamander genus *Pseudobranchus* (Sirenidae). *Copeia* 1993:39–47.

Myers, G. S. 1950. The systematic status of *Hyla septentrionalis*, the large treefrog of the Florida Keys, the Bahamas and Cuba. *Copeia* 1950:203–214.

Myers, S. 1977. Geographic distribution: *Osteopilus septentrionalis*. *Herpetol. Rev.* 8:38.

Neill, W. T. 1958. The occurrence of amphibians and reptiles in saltwater areas, and a bibliography. *Bull. Mar. Sci. Gulf Caribb.* 8:1–97.

Noble, G. K. 1927. The value of life history data in the study of the evolution of the Amphibia. *Ann. Rev. N.Y. Acad. Sci.* 33:31–128.

Owre, O. T. 1973. A consideration of the exotic avifauna of southeastern Florida. *Wilson Bull.* 85:491–500.

Parker, G. G., G. E. Ferguson, and S. K. Love. 1955. *Water Resources of Southeastern Florida*. Geological Survey water-supply paper 1255, U.S. G.P.O., Washington, D.C.

Pearce, E. A., and G. Smith. 1990. *World Weather Guide*. Times Books, Random House, London.

Peterson, W., R. Garrett, and J. P. Lantz. 1952. The mating period of the giant tree frog *Hyla dominicensis*. *Herpetologica* 8:63.

Pimm, S. L. 1989. Theories of predicting success and impact of introduced species. *In* J. A. Drake, H. A. Mooney, F. di Castri, R. H. Groves, F. J. Kruger, M. Rejmanek, and M. Williamson (eds.), *Biological Invasions: A Global Perspective*, 351–367. John Wiley and Sons, New York.

———. 1991. *The Balance of Nature? Ecological Issues in the Conservation of Species and Communities*. Univ. Chicago Press, Chicago.

Powell, R., R. J. Passaro, and R. W. Henderson. 1992. Noteworthy herpetological records from Saint Maarten, Netherlands, Antilles. *Caribb. J. Sci.* 28:234–235.

Renkonen, O. 1938. Statisch-okologische Untersuchungen uberdie terrestiche kaferwelt der finnischen bruchmoore. *Ann. Zool. Soc. Zool.-Bot. Fenn. 'Vanamo'* 6:1–231.

Robertson, W. B., Jr. 1955. An analysis of the breeding-bird populations of tropical Florida in relation to the vegetation. Ph.D. diss. University of Illinois, Urbana.

Rossi, J. V. 1981. *Bufo marinus* in Florida: some natural history and its impact on native vertebrates. M.S. thesis. University of South Florida, Tampa.

Ruiz Garcia, F. N. 1987. *Anfibios de Cuba*. Editorial Gente Nueva, Havana.

Salthe, S. N., and W. E. Duellman. 1973. Quantitative constraints associated with reproductive mode in anurans. *In* J. L. Vial (ed.), *Evolutionary Biology of the*

Anurans: Contemporary Research on Major Problems, 229–249. Univ. Missouri Press, Columbia.

Savidge, J. A. 1987. Extinction of an island avifauna by an introduced snake. *Ecology* 68:660–668.

Schlegel, H. 1837–1844. *Abbildungen neuer oder unvollstandig bekannter Amphibien, nach der Natur oder dem Leben entwrofen, herausgegeben und mit erlauternden Texte begleitet.* Dusseldorf.

Schwartz, A. 1952. *Hyla septentrionalis* Dumeril and Bibron on the Florida mainland. *Copeia* 1952:117–118.

———. 1968. The geckos (*Sphaerodactylus*) of the southern Bahamas islands. *Ann. Carnegie Mus.* 39:227–271.

Schwartz, A., and R. W. Henderson. 1991. *Amphibians and Reptiles of the West Indies: Descriptions, Distributions, and Natural History.* Univ. Florida Press, Gainesville.

Schwartz, A., and L. H. Ogren. 1956. A collection of reptiles and amphibians from Cuba, with the description of two new forms. *Herpetologica* 12:91–110.

Schwartz, A., and R. Thomas. 1975. *A Checklist of West Indian Amphibians and Reptiles.* Spec. Publ. No. 1, Carnegie Museum of Natural History, Pittsburgh.

Sexton, O. J., and K. M. Brown. 1977. The reproductive cycle of an iguanid lizard *Anolis sagrei*, from Belize. *J. Natural History* 11:241–250.

Siebert, E. A., H. B. Lillywhite, and R. J. Wassersug. 1974. Cranial co-ossification in frogs: relationship to rate of evaporative loss. *Physiol. Zool.* 47:261–265.

Somma, L. A., and D. M. Crawford. 1993. Geographic distribution, *Osteopilus septentrionalis. Herpetological Review* 24:153.

Stejneger, L. 1905. Batrachians and land reptiles of the Bahama Islands. *In* G. B. Shattuck (ed.), *The Bahama Islands. A Report of the Bahama Expedition Sent Out by the Geographical Society of Baltimore,* 329–242. Macmillan, New York.

Stevenson, H. M. 1976. *Vertebrates of Florida.* Univ. Press Florida, Gainesville.

Tebeau, C. W. 1968. *Man in the Everglades.* Univ. Miami Press, Coral Gables, Fla.

Townsend, J. H., J. M. Eaton, R. Powell, J. S. Parmerlee Jr., and R. W. Henderson. 2000. Cuban treefrogs (*Osteopilus septentrionalis*) in Anguilla, Lesser Antilles. *Caribb. J. Sci.* 36:326–328.

Trapido, H. 1947. Range extension of *Hyla septentrionalis* in Florida. *Herpetologica* 3:190.

Trueb, L. 1966. Morphology and development in the skull of *Hyla septentrionalis. Copeia* 1966:562–573.

———. 1970. Evolutionary relationships of casque-head treefrogs with co-ossified skulls (Family Hylidae). *Univ. Kans. Publ. Mus. Nat. Hist.* 18:547–716.

Trueb, L., and M. J. Tyler. 1974. Systematics and evolution of the Greater Antillean hylid frogs. *Occ. Pap. Mus. Nat. Hist. Univ. Kans.*, Lawrence 24:1–60.

Tschudi, J. J. von. 1838. *Classification der batrachier, mit beruksichtigung der fossilen.* Neuchatel.

Vitt, L. J. 1986. Reproductive tactics of sympatric gekkonid lizards with a comment on the evolutionary and ecological consequences of invariant clutch size. *Copeia* 1986:773–786.

Voss, R. 1975. Notes on the introduced gecko *Hemidactylus garnotii* in south Florida. *Fla. Sci.* 38:174.

Wilson, L. D., and L. Porras. 1983. The ecological impact of man on the south Florida herpetofauna. *Univ. Kans. Mus. Nat. Hist. Spec. Publ.* 9:1–89.

Wood, R. A. 1996. *The Weather Almanac.* Gale Research, New York.

Wright, A. H., and A. A. Wright. 1949. *Handbook of Frogs and Toads of the United States and Canada.* Comstock, Ithaca, N.Y.

Wygoda, M. L. 1982. *Low evaporative water loss in North American treefrogs.* Ph.D. diss. University of Florida, Gainesville.

Wygoda, M. L. 1984. Low cutaneous water loss in arboreal frogs. *Physiol. Zool.* 57:329–337.

Young, F. N., and J. R. Zimmerman. 1956. Variations in temperature in small aquatic situations. *Ecology* 37:609–611.

Zajiceck, D., and M. Mauri Mendez. 1969. Hemo-parasitos de algunas animales de Cuba. *Poeyana* Ser. A. 66:1–10.

Zug, G. R., and P. B. Zug. 1979. The marine toad, *Bufo marinus:* a natural history resume of native populations. *Smithson. Contrib. Zool.* 284:1–58.

Index

W. E. Meshaka Jr. is senior curator of zoology and botany at the State Museum of Pennsylvania in Harrisburg. His interests are in the ecology of amphibians and reptiles and in colonization theory.